Ted Cu

A LOVE THAT LAUGHS

Lighten Up, Cut Loose
and Enjoy Life Together

TYNDALE HOUSE PUBLISHERS
CAROL STREAM, ILLINOIS

FOCUS ON THE FAMILY®

Contents

Acknowledgments

Thank you, Alex Field, for your friendship and leadership. This is my seventh book with you: six as my publisher and now as my literary agent. I trust your expertise completely.

Everyone at Focus on the Family is like family to me. Your partnership over the years validates my message and ministry. Thank you to Jim Daly, John Fuller, Greg and Erin Smalley, Heather Dedrick, Steve Johnson, Larry Weeden, Beth Robinson, and Sandra Henderson.

My comedian friends Paul Harris, Jason Earls, John Branyan, and Johnnie W. inspired many of the laughs throughout this book. You four heard my comedy set multiple times, and your feedback is invaluable. You are generous veterans and mentors to me.

Doug Fields, Matt Engel, Ted Lowe, Scott Kedersha, John McGee, Phil Gungor, Gary Thomas, and Tim Popadic are dear friends and champions in marriage ministry. I learn much from them.

Woodland Hills Family Church is my home. Amy and I can't imagine serving anywhere else. To the congregation, staff, elders, and teaching team, you all serve incredibly well. This allows each one of us to pursue our passions, gifts, and calling.

To my daughter, Corynn Mae, our entire family lives for your laugh. Your laughter is the most contagious in our family. When you lose control, so do we.

To my son, Carson Matthew, you are the last-born comedian of our family. Not a day goes by without a few laughs from your antics, jokes, and quick recalls of famous movie lines.

Amy Cunningham, my goal in life is to make you laugh. You are the reason I do comedy. I know if a punch line, impersonation, or teaching point makes you laugh, then it will work around the world. Our laughs get better with age. My goal is to increase our laughter ratio and score with each passing year.

Introduction

My wife, Amy, is a foodie. Her favorite restaurants serve small portions over many courses, and you never have to use the same utensil twice. I prefer large portions served all at once, and I'm good with using the same fork for the entire meal. You would think these differences frustrate us, but they don't. We decided a long time ago to find fun in every nook and cranny of our marriage.

Our foodie differences first surfaced at a fancy restaurant in New York City. When we walked in, I knew immediately I would leave hungry. It was the type of restaurant some would call a "four forker."

The friendly host seated us at a table near the front window. We had a welcoming view of the garden terrace, and plenty of privacy. It was cute, cozy, and romantic.

The waiter approached with a thick wood plank and presented us with two mint leaves. My immediate question was, "Is that the salad?" He assured me it was not.

He invited us to each take a leaf and rub it over our lips, under our noses, and around our chins. Amy was all in, but I hesitated. All I did was hold my leaf and stare at the waiter.

"I grew up in Illinois where we grew produce, but we never rubbed it on our faces," I said in jest. Our waiter didn't laugh. Come on, shouldn't rubbing herbs on your face be something a couple does in private? This was certainly the most awkward moment I've ever experienced in a restaurant.

The waiter stood there waiting for me to cleanse my palate, so I gave him a show he would not soon forget. I took a bath with that mint leaf, rubbing it all over my body, then discarded the wilted leaf on the plank. He stared in silent rebuke, took our order, and left in a huff.

The waiter wasn't amused, but Amy sure was. Amy's belly laugh reassured me she knew how awkward this was for me. She appreciates how I play through the pain. No matter where we are, no matter what we are doing, we try to prioritize fun and laughter.

Amy and I turned our fancy-restaurant, leaf-rubbing date into what is known in comedy circles as a *callback*. Now every time we go to my favorite restaurant, Le Cracker Barrel, getting her to laugh is easy. All I have to do is reach over, grab a piece of broccoli off of her plate, and rub it on my cheek. I sometimes get a smile, but if I add some physical comedy, I can get a chuckle or even a belly laugh.

The Callback

The callback is one of my favorite comedy skills. Great comedy is about surprising and shocking the brain. When a comedian shares a punch line you didn't anticipate, your mind is shocked into laughter. The callback shocks the brain with two thoughts, "I didn't see that coming," and "I should have seen that coming."

Writing comedy is similar to writing a sermon, speech, or research paper. It takes discipline. The mistake a lot of public speakers make is thinking that comedy is best when spontaneous. Not true. It may look spontaneous, but it is not. Good comedy is written, edited, practiced, and edited some more. Let that be part of your journey as a couple working through this book. Be intentional.

While writing great material takes discipline, the formula for writing comedy is simple: Establish a premise, then deliver the punch line. Skilled comedians establish a single premise, then layer multiple punch lines after it. For example, comedian Jim Gaffigan layers dozens of punch lines behind the premises of cake, bacon, and Hot Pockets. We laugh and subliminally think, *I didn't see that coming, but I should have.*

The callback takes a punch line from earlier in the set and delivers it off of a new premise later. It is a joke for a second time in a different context. For example, my good friend comedian Paul Harris has a bit on bull riding in his set. He talks about his friend Rusty, who talked him into bull riding for the first time. Paul says, "Ask the fellas in here, they'll tell you, a good friend can talk you into doing stupid stuff."

Twenty minutes later, Paul shares the story of peeing on his grandpa's electric fence. As the crowd roars with laughter, he says, "It didn't feel like Rusty said it would." Paul's special, "Y'all Haul," is available on iTunes and Apple Music. I recommend it. He is a comedy genius who knows how to use the callback.

When I first learned about the callback, I thought to myself, "Every couple needs callbacks." You know, like inside jokes that only the two of you get. Jokes that resurface in the recurring moments and issues of your marriage. What would married life look like in your home if you turned every nagging frustration, irritation, and conflict into a callback? What if we had inside jokes that changed the way we communicate, date, commit to projects around the house, flirt, eat, watch movies, drive, park, and parent? That's my plan for your journey through *A Love That Laughs*.

Throughout this book, I hope to share with you how to craft callbacks in all areas of your marriage. With practice, you can turn what used to be frustrating conversations into playful banter. Let's turn those differences that wear you out into opportunities for mutual laughs.

We often refer to the funny bone, but I think humor is more like a muscle—it requires a workout. It may be painful and uncomfortable at first, but the payoff is worth the work. For that reason, I'll be encouraging you to recruit a couple of friends on this journey. Think of them as workout partners, helping you commit to lifelong love and laughs.

I've been traveling the past few years on the Date Night Comedy Tour, combining my passion to help couples thrive with my love for making people laugh. On tour, I invite couples to share their callbacks. One of my all-time favorite callbacks is from a friend we met at Kanakuk Family Kamp in Branson, Missouri. He shared this with a room full of couples and received sustained laughter. Little did he know, I would share this with thousands of couples on tour and get the biggest laugh in my stand-up set.

In this callback, my friend left for work without fixing a running toilet. Like most couples, it's the little things that wear on a marriage. I call that the daily grind. And it doesn't get more daily grind than a running toilet. Call me chivalrous, but I still think the man should do the dirty work. That's not to say a woman can't, but men don't shoot and kill food each day and drag it home like we used to. We must find other ways to be the hero. If fixing a running toilet brings out the cape, then so be it.

My friend's wife called him to report the problem with the toilet, and he talked her through the easy fix.

"Honey, take the lid off of the tank on top of the toilet," he coached her. With the phone pinned between her cheek and shoulder, she proceeded.

He continued, "Okay, if you look at the bottom of the tank, you should see the chain wrapped around the suction ball. Reach down . . ."

"Ewwww! Yuck! I'm not reaching in there. Disgusting!" she interrupted.

"Babe, it's clean water, like water that comes out of the tap," he reassured her.

After some convincing, she agreed to do it. Right before her hand hit the water she asked, "Am I going to get electrocuted?"

The husband held back his laughter. Good move. Some things are funny hours, days, or weeks later, but not in the moment. Timing is a key to great comedy. You may need to give it some time.

"Am I going to get electrocuted?" has the potential for a great callback, but that is not the callback this couple now uses in their marriage. Their callback is in how the husband answered that question:

"Whoa, good catch, honey. You've got to unplug the toilet first," he said.

I can hear it now.

"The garage door ain't working."

"Did you unplug it?"

"The baby won't go to sleep."

"Unplug her."

"I'm not feeling all that well."

"May be time to pull the plug."

The layers of marital comedy are endless on the callback.

In the back of this book we have a Callback Journal for you to record the callbacks in your marriage. As you work through the activities at the end of each chapter, jot down the ones that really stick, and carry them with you through your married life.

Obviously, *A Love That Laughs* is not competing with *The Five Love Languages* by Gary Chapman, *Sacred Marriage* by Gary Thomas, *Love and Respect* by Dr. Emerson Eggerichs, or *The Meaning of Marriage* by Timothy Keller. I revere those marriage classics but I have a completely different mission.

For a change of pace, read this book in between the more serious marriage books and studies. Allow humor and laughter to help you and your spouse lighten up and enjoy life together.

A Love That Laughs is your guide to pursuing deliberate laughter. Be intentional and laugh together.

CHAPTER I

Your Laughter Score

Enjoy life with the wife whom you love.

ECCLESIASTES 9:9

---

*We cannot really love anybody
with whom we never laugh.*

AGNES REPPLIER

A MARRIAGE THAT LAUGHS LASTS. Couples who use laughter
to manage stress and work through difficult conversations
not only enjoy higher levels of marital satisfaction, but stay
together longer. Laughter bonds us, eases tension, defuses
anger, lightens the mood, and makes us more attractive and
relatable. Our laughter signals to family, friends, and strangers, "This couple enjoys life together."

Amy and I have a laugh-to-conflict ratio of about 100:1.
Laughter has always been important to us, but some seasons require greater intentionality. I asked Amy on a date
one night, "Do you feel we laugh enough?" It was during a

season when the pressures of ministry and family weighed heavy on us.

She said, "I think our laughs outweigh our frustrations about one hundred to one." Voilà. *Abracadabra*. And just like that our laughter ratio appeared. But we didn't stop evaluating our laughter quotient there. What if we could measure laughs throughout the day?

Comedians measure the effectiveness of their comedy sets with a laughs-per-minute ratio. Three to five laughs per minute makes for great comedy. The next time you say or do something that prompts spontaneous laughter in your spouse, don't settle for a single chuckle. Dig deeper. Go for more. I hope this book gives you some ideas and maybe a little more confidence to increase your laughs-per-minute ratio, but that is not the only goal. The goal is to increase your laughs per day. Start by answering these two questions:

How many *laughs per day* do you and your spouse exchange?

What is your *laughs-per-day* goal while reading this book?

I love asking friends and strangers, "On any given day, how many times do you and your spouse laugh together?"

It encourages me when I hear, "We laugh a lot," "Dozens of times a day," and "Too many times to count." It's the answers of "Rarely," "Not nearly enough," and "I can't remember the last time" that confirm my marriage ministry calling: *To help couples laugh and enjoy life together.*

My personality leans toward humor naturally. It's always

been a part of my teaching and pastoral ministry. And almost twenty-five years into ministry, I'm leaning into laughter now more than ever. Why? Because I see the medicine that it truly is. It helps husbands receive difficult truths at marriage conferences. Shoot, it even helps wives get their husbands to marriage events. It's part of connecting with the congregation when I teach, visiting folks in the hospital, officiating at weddings, and helping couples through challenging seasons.

I've been accused of using too much humor in sermons and ministry. That's tough, but fair. Charles Spurgeon was accused of the very same thing. His quip to that comment has become mine: "If you only knew how much I hold back."

Choose Laughter, Fun, and Attention over Hard Work

Have you heard the all-too-common idea about marriage that sounds something like "Marriage is difficult, painful, grueling, and hard"? I hate when that tone pervades and dominates a marriage. This should not be. God didn't give you your spouse to "beat you down and suck the life out of you so you can be more like Jesus." You don't need to choose between a happy life and a happy marriage. You can have both at the same time. One way to enjoy life together is by prioritizing laughter in marriage.

When Amy and I first married, we held hands as we walked everywhere. Sitting in restaurants, movies, and church, we rested our hands on each other's legs. Lots of touching, gazing, and talking.

As a pastor, I preach often on the joys of marriage. I can still picture members of our congregation rolling their eyes at my gushiness. One deacon of a church approached me after one such impassioned message and said, "Don't worry, Ted, you'll get over it."

You know what? He was wrong. Amy and I have our share of struggles like every couple, but we can say without hesitation that marriage gets better with time and attention. Every year we enjoy our marriage more and more. We proved that deacon wrong.

Instead of saying, "Marriage takes hard work," we say, "Marriage requires our attention." We've given our marriage our undivided attention for the past twenty-three years and it has paid off. We give our marriage attention and fun. Have we had difficult seasons? Of course, but we don't allow the struggles of marriage to become the main emphasis.

While writing this book, I prayed for your marriage. I asked the Lord to help you find the humor in your differences, personalities, communication, commitment, families of origin, and even conflicts.

You need to choose laughter rather than wait for it. Most of us enjoy spontaneous laughter but struggle with voluntary laughter. Spontaneous laughter waits for something funny to happen. Voluntary laughter chooses the humorous side of things and makes the laughs happen.

Humor is a choice, not just an outcome. You get to decide

your way into laughter. As a couple, you choose whether an activity, outing, date night, or event is fun or frustrating. Where you are and what you are doing are factors in the equation, but they are not the summation of a good time. Stop waiting for humor and start creating it.

For example, have you experienced a day when everything went wrong? Everyone and everything seemed to be working against you to the point that it was stupid funny? You simply shake your head and say in jest, "What else could go wrong?" Every bad thing that happens to you after that question is one more punch line or callback to the day. It gives you and your spouse one more fun story to share.

When fun and laughter is an outcome rather than a choice, the quality of your marriage is determined by the words and actions of others. When fun and laughter is a choice and not an outcome, the quality of your marriage is determined by your attitude and actions.

You may resist this idea of deciding on laughter and think, *Yeah, this is all well and good, but it takes two people to make marriage fun.* I submit to you that it often only takes one spouse to get the ball rolling. Start with you. Decisions have power. Decide for yourself (not your spouse) to loosen up, not take yourself so seriously, and enjoy what life throws at you. You may say, "Is this even biblical?" What did James mean when through the inspiration of the Holy Spirit he wrote in James 1:2, "Count it all joy, my brothers, when you meet trials of various kinds"? Isn't laughter an expression of joy? I say yes. When trials hit your marriage, take the first step and invite some lightheartedness into your union. Making marriage fun is up to you.

Ecclesiastes 9:9 (NIV) says, "Enjoy life with your wife, whom you love, all the days of this meaningless life that God has given you under the sun—all your meaningless days. For this is your lot in life and in your toilsome labor under the sun." Life is difficult, challenging, and painful, but you have a spouse to journey with you through it all. Your spouse, not the grind, is your companion. You do not need to choose between life and spouse. Choose both.

British neuroscientist Sophie Scott believes that the origins of laughter are found in social interactions and that is why we are thirty times more likely to laugh with others than by ourselves.[1] Laughter brings us closer together and creates a longing for us to stay close for the long haul. It is for that reason that after a night of laughter with close friends we say something like, "That was so good. I needed that. I can't wait for us to be together again." Laughter creates this bond in marriage, too.

We can't always escape the tough stuff in life, nor should we. Yet laughter can bring a brief pause to a difficult time and give us what we need to make it through. As Milton Berle once said, "Laughter is an instant vacation." You can take it anytime without asking your boss. It's free. You don't need childcare or someone to water the plants.

Your marriage needs a daily break, free from serious conversations about budgeting, parenting, jobs, and household chores. All it takes is a few minutes of spontaneity to lighten up and inject a little fun into your everyday routines, mishaps, and occasional rubs.

Laughter is found while you're stuck in traffic, standing in line at the DMV, and even eating a holiday meal with crazy relatives. It's up to you. Will you make the choice? Will you turn everyday moments into lighter moments? While standing in line at the DMV, break into a spontaneous dance to a familiar tune. While waiting in traffic, turn on the radio and belt out a song. Better yet, turn the radio off and belt out a classic and invite your spouse to join in. If you can't sing or dance, that's even better. Uncoordinated dancing and out-of-tune singing are guaranteed laughs. Make it your goal to get your spouse to smile, chuckle, or even belly laugh.

The Sixth Love Language

One of the bestselling marriage books of all time is *The Five Love Languages* by Dr. Gary Chapman. A person's love language refers to how that person likes to receive love from others. A love language can also refer to how we like to show love to others. Dr. Chapman identifies five love languages: physical touch, words of affirmation, gift giving, acts of service, and quality time.

Not to second-guess Dr. Chapman, but I wholeheartedly believe the sixth love language is laughter. Laughing together is a way to show genuine love and care for each other. My wife shows me love when she laughs with me. I show her love when I make her laugh. If your love language is gift giving, that doesn't excuse you from touching, sharing kind words, serving, or spending time with your spouse.

Some might say food is the sixth love language. A strong case could be made for that. I have plenty of friends and family who are constantly bringing me homemade goodies or inviting me over for a meal. I believe food is my mother-in-law's love language. She not only loves cooking for us, she watches us eat and finds great joy in our responses. I show her love by eating some foods I don't care for, going back for seconds, and requesting certain foods for our next family gathering. She always delivers.

The same is true for laughter. If laughter is not your love language, you're not off the hook. Laughter may be your spouse's love language, but not yours. If that's the case, engage in humor as an act of love. Ask for a joke at the end of an exhausting day. Request a funny dance move. Laugh when it wasn't funny. That's the equivalent of going back for seconds of a dish you didn't care for.

You've heard it said, "People don't care what you know until they know that you care." Laughter is a great way to love and care for your spouse. Amy and I use laughter to both connect with each other and to know we're connected. It is a great barometer for our marriage.

Are you ready to get your laugh on? It's time to get serious about laughter.

Your Laughter Score

Each chapter of this book ends with a section called *Your Laughter Score*. There are two activities to initiate laughter in marriage. Some activities will hit you stronger than others. Some will stretch you. Some may become a regular activity at home. All of them, with valiant effort, will evoke some response from your spouse.

The activities and scoring are meant to be fun. Banter over the quality of the laughter from each activity. That's like a bonus round, laughing over how you laughed. There are four factors to consider with *Your Laughter Score*.

First, laughter builds from small to big. There are many different types of laughter. For scoring, you will use the following ten types of laughter, slightly adapted from the *Journal of Nursing Jocularity*. You may need to mark this page so you can refer back to the definitions in forthcoming chapters. Also, if you read this together or your spouse is in the same room, demonstrate each of the following so you have a visual for the laugh activities to come. Here are the ten in order:

1. **Smirk:** Half-smile, slight, often fleeting upturning of the corners of the mouth, completely voluntary and controllable.

2. **Smile:** Silent, voluntary, and controllable, starts to use more facial muscles; begins to release endorphins.

3. **Snicker:** First emergence of sound with facial muscles, but still controllable (if you hold in a snicker, it builds up gas).

4. **Giggle:** Not yet considered laugh out loud, but efforts to suppress it tend to increase its strength.

5. **Chuckle:** Controllable and voluntary, involves chest muscles with deeper pitch.

6. **Cackle:** First involuntary stage; pitch is higher and body begins to rock, spine extends and flexes, with an upturning of head.

7. **Belly Laugh:** Also known as a guffaw, it's a loud and boisterous laugh. Full-body response—feet stomp, arms wave, thighs are slapped, torso rocks, sound is deep and loud; may result in free-flowing tears, increased heart rate, and breathlessness.

8. **Howl:** Volume and pitch rise higher and higher and the body becomes more animated.

9. **Shriek:** Greater intensity than howl; sense of helplessness and vulnerability.

10. **Die Laughing:** Hard time breathing, instance of total helplessness; a brief, physically intense, transcendent experience; having died, we thereafter report

a refreshing moment of breathlessness and exhaustion with colors more vivid and everything sparkling; everything is renewed.[2]

Second, there are a ton of points to earn. One of our family's favorite rides at Disneyland is Toy Story Midway Mania! You throw digital rings, darts, and pies at carnival-style games to earn points. With little skill, over 100,000 points is possible. That ride and game is always a shot in the arm for this competitive dad. *Your Laughter Score* gives you the opportunity to earn 250,000 points by the end of the book. Let's go big so no spouse finishes the book feeling like a loser. Even if your laughter score is a mere 100,000 points, others will be impressed. Every spouse will finish the book with a score to brag about.

Third, there are no points for trying. If your attempt at humor falls flat, that's zero points. No participation trophies or ribbons here. You must get a response to score points, but you'll be shocked at how fast you get points on the board. With your whole heart into it, I don't believe you'll have many "fell flat" scores.

Fourth, you and your spouse determine the scores. You can determine your own score on each activity or decide it together. Again, if the banter over scores leads to a higher score, feel free to use that number instead. Remember, the laughter, not the activity, is the most important factor. Each chapter ends with the following scale for each attempt at laughter:

My attempt at humor . . .

Fell flat ....0 points
Made my spouse smirk .... 1,000 points
Made my spouse smile .... 2,000 points
Made my spouse snicker .... 3,000 points
Made my spouse giggle .... 4,000 points
Made my spouse chuckle .... 5,000 points
Made my spouse cackle .... 6,000 points
Made my spouse belly laugh .... 7,000 points
Made my spouse howl .... 8,000 points
Made my spouse shriek .... 9,000 points
Made my spouse die laughing .... 10,000 points

The final chapter of the book is called "Extra Credit: Ten Fast, Easy, and Free Ways to Make Your Spouse Laugh" for a possible 100,000 extra-credit points. Husbands will thrive on the competitive nature of this book.

After each activity and score, there is a place to jot notes on how to improve. This is how you get better at the comedy of marriage. Take notes on your delivery, timing, shortcomings, messed-up words, and surprises that hit you along the way. You'd be shocked to know how many bits that comedians discover in the moment on stage. Unplanned material and the audience's response to it make for great lessons and future material. Don't let those moments pass you by. Write them down. If you're going through this book with other couples, share not only your scores, but also your lessons learned.

Here's what shocked me the most about these activities. Just mentioning to Amy some of the activities in this book scored me 5,000 points. *What?* Discussion of the activity alone generated a chuckle.

For that reason, Amy insisted that I add conversation starters for spouses who want to laugh but not compete. She says this has more to do with the Enneagram than it does laughter. Due to my wife's passion for the Enneagram, there will be no jokes in this book about the Enneagram. She says I know just enough about it to be dangerous. I say I know just enough about it to be funny.

Nonetheless, each chapter will have conversation starters for a few more laughs. In this section there's no need to keep score. Just roll with them. Laughter may be the one skill you didn't know your marriage was missing.

Your Laughter Score

For a possible 20,000 points, start with some low-hanging fruit.

1. Belt It Out. Singing at the top of your lungs works for almost everyone. It works best when you don't know the lyrics and you sing off-key. Turn up the radio, make up the words, and belt it out with passion and conviction. Your spouse will appreciate and maybe even applaud your attempt. A verse or chorus will do. If you really want to step it up, invite your spouse to join you.

My attempt at humor . . .

Fell flat...0 points
Made my spouse smirk.............................1,000 points
Made my spouse smile...............................2,000 points
Made my spouse snicker.............................3,000 points
Made my spouse giggle.............................4,000 points
Made my spouse chuckle............................5,000 points
Made my spouse cackle ....6,000 points
Made my spouse belly laugh.......................7,000 points
Made my spouse howl ....8,000 points
Made my spouse shriek ....9,000 points
Made my spouse die laughing..................10,000 points

_____ Her Score _____ His Score

The next time I attempt this humor, I will

_____

2. Get Jiggy with It. Uninhibited dancing ties for first place with singing when it comes to making others laugh. This one gets a little more vulnerable, but like singing, the worse you are the greater the laughs. Low risk, but high rewards. Get out your phone when your spouse least expects it and play Michael Jackson's "Billie Jean" or Billy Ray Cyrus's "Achy Breaky Heart" and give the performance of your life.

My attempt at humor . . .

Fell flat..0 points
Made my spouse smirk.............................1,000 points
Made my spouse smile..............................2,000 points
Made my spouse snicker...........................3,000 points
Made my spouse giggle.............................4,000 points
Made my spouse chuckle..........................5,000 points
Made my spouse cackle.............................6,000 points
Made my spouse belly laugh......................7,000 points
Made my spouse howl...............................8,000 points
Made my spouse shriek.............................9,000 points
Made my spouse die laughing..................10,000 points

_____ Her Score _____ His Score

The next time I attempt this humor, I will

_____

Write your scores on page 205, too.

Conversation Starters and a Few More Laughs

- What sign best describes you on a bad day? And why?

  A. Proceed with Caution
  B. Beware of Dog
  C. No Trespassing
  D. Pass with Care

- Name a time laughter really helped when you had a bad day.

- What is the number one barrier to enjoying life together in your marriage?

- Is there an issue or unresolved conflict that you see turning into laughs instead of constant frustration?

- Do you believe you are humorous?

CHAPTER 2

Thirty-Eight
"We Need More of That"
Benefits of Laughter

A joyful heart is good medicine.

PROVERBS 17:22

Laughter is the most beautiful and beneficial therapy
God ever granted humanity.

PASTOR CHUCK SWINDOLL

THE MORE I STUDY the benefits of laughter, the more of it I want for my marriage. The more we laugh, the less we fight. The more we laugh, the more we want others to join us. The more we laugh, the better we feel. The more we laugh, the better we get at it. The more we laugh, the more productive we are in other areas of life. Laughter is powerful and beneficial for our overall wellness.

I've spent the past three years studying laughter. The studying is fun, but the practice is better. I catch myself trying crazy and outside-the-box ways of making Amy laugh. When an attempt fails and she is not amused, I don't quit. I give her some space, work on my timing, edit my content, and try again. Humor benefits our marriage mentally, emotionally, physically, relationally, and spiritually. Laughter makes us healthier and happier.

Jim Gaffigan is our favorite comedian. Known as the King of Clean Comedy, Jim proves that you don't need to use the f-word to get a laugh. His comedy specials influenced my teaching style a few years back. One pastor recently said to me, "Not only do you watch Jim Gaffigan, you study Jim Gaffigan."

In April 2017, Jim's wife, Jeannie, was diagnosed with a brain tumor. One year later, after the tumor was successfully removed, they were both interviewed on nationwide TV.[1] It was a touching interview. From diagnosis to surgery and through recovery, Jim and Jeannie used humor to cope as a couple. They both believe you can find humor in almost any situation. Jeannie spent hours in MRI machines and wrote jokes while holding perfectly still. As a mother of five, Jeannie found that the MRI was the only time she had to herself. Her first request to Jim after a test or procedure was to write down some of the material she thought of for his act.

Jim has a brain tumor bit in his comedy special "Noble Ape." In it he jokes, "Laughter is the best medicine, but only after you take real medicine." This professional comedy couple not only uses laughter to encourage others, they found its benefits helpful for themselves through one of the most challenging times of their marriage.

Laughter has benefits for your mind, body, heart, relationships, and walk with God. Read through the following benefits of laughter and allow yourself to have some "I've never thought of that before" moments. Also, consider these benefits for your marriage by sharing with each other, "We need more of that." The following thirty-eight benefits are conversation starters for a deeper understanding of laughter and of each other.

The Mental Benefits of Laughter

1. Laughter sharpens the mind. God created humor and wired us to respond accordingly. Your mind is the control center for laughter. When you hear a joke or a funny story, something happens inside of you that God planned at creation. Humor aids in keeping your mind working. The prefrontal cortex in your frontal lobe works overtime when you hear a joke. Your brain processes punch lines in its pleasure-and-reward center, which in turn triggers your laugh. Humor and laughter are not passive activities. They require the brain to get a workout.[2]

2. Laughter coats the brain with dopamine. Say no to drugs and yes to laughter. Some seek relief from the problems of life through substances, but God wired your brain to manufacture and release its own stress reliever. The workout you get while laughing releases dopamine, which enhances pleasure; serotonin, to put us in a better mood; and endorphins, to regulate pain and stress.[3]

3. Laughter increases long-term memory retention. Marketers call this "emotional linkage." Commercials that evoke deep emotions connect us to the message. I can still sing "I'd like to teach the world to sing in perfect harmony" from the commercials in the seventies because the theme of unity and peace struck a chord during the Cold War. Its message, theme, and jingle seared themselves into my mind and never left.

Humor works the exact same way. Thirty-five years later, I still remember "Where's the beef?" That Wendy's commercial is forever in my frontal lobe. Mental functions increase when our memory is jostled by humor. How many moments of laughter do you and your spouse share and say something like, "Do you remember the time we . . . ?" "A few years ago the same thing happened to us and we . . . ." "This isn't the first time we've done this." Laughter sears moments into our minds and helps us recall them as well.

4. Humor helps us learn. Just as laughter helps us recall memories, it also helps us retain content and information. As a preacher and communicator, I use this benefit often. Laughter is medicine, but it also helps other medicines go down.

I had a history teacher in high school who used sound effects to teach history. He had sounds for gusts of wind and storms as he taught about the hardships early settlers faced. He was a walking soundtrack too, singing familiar tunes off-key to teach the lessons. Our senior year English teacher did the same. He required impersonations from us as we read *Macbeth* and English accents when we read *Romeo and Juliet*. It's amazing how much more you remember when you're laughing.

This is why I use so much laughter at couples' conferences. Men don't show up super excited for three to four sessions of marriage content. Working on their marriage on Friday night is not at the top of their list. That's why my favorite line to hear at the end of the first session is "This is not at all what I expected." They're receiving content as they would from other marriage speakers, but the delivery is fun and memorable.

5. Humor opens the mind to new ideas. Neurohumorist Karyn Buxman believes humor has the power to save the world. She recounts the story, told by economist John Kenneth Galbraith, in which a joke may have staved off war. During the Cuban Missile Crisis in 1962, the United States of America was on the brink of war with the Soviet Union. Most believe it is the closest we have ever come to a nuclear holocaust. With Soviet missiles in Cuba, ninety miles from American shores, the conflict escalated quickly.

American and Soviet delegates met to discuss possible de-escalation of the nuclear threat. One of the Soviet delegates broke the tension by making a joke:

> Q: "What's the difference between capitalism and communism?"
> A: "In capitalism, man exploits man. In communism, it's the other way around."[4]

I don't know if that joke saved the world, but I'd like to think it helped and opened the group to consider new ways forward. Laughter has the power to bring clarity. Steve Bhaerman says, "The surprise of humor stops ordinary one-track thinking in its 'track' and there is an opening for new ideas and new possibilities."[5]

6. Laughter diverts your attention from stressful issues. A quick chuckle shifts our concerns to the back burners. After a stressful day, when you are tempted to replay or rehearse that bad meeting or some critical email, try to find the humor in it. Ask yourself, "What will this matter in five or ten years?" I find that question helps me look for the lighter moments in conflict and troubles. You and your spouse, after some time passes, can help one another find these lighter moments in hard times.

When I was twenty-seven years old, I shared a terrible church experience with my mentor, Dr. Gary Smalley. He laughed. Not at me, but in reflecting on a similar situation he'd had thirty years earlier. He then asked me, "Have you praised your Father in heaven for this trial?" My answer was "No." He said, "You should, because you will be grateful for this lesson." He was a master at laughing at trials, knowing the fruit they produce down the road.

The Emotional Benefits of Laughter

7. **Humor refreshes us.** Emotionally healthy couples experience a wide range of emotions. Some seasons bring sorrow and mourning. Other seasons bring joy and laughter. To remain in one season all of the time is not emotionally healthy. Winter all year long is not beneficial for your marriage. After a month of below-freezing days, I'm ready for a new season with warmer temperatures. If your marriage is going through a cold spell, it's time to ask God for a new, refreshing season. According to Ecclesiastes 3:1-4, there are God-appointed times and seasons:

> For everything there is a season,
>   and a time for every matter under heaven:
> a time to be born, and a time to die;
>   a time to plant, and a time to pluck up what is
>   planted;
> a time to kill, and a time to heal;
>   a time to break down, and a time to build up;
> a time to weep, and a time to laugh;
>   a time to mourn, and a time to dance.

Laughter is a new season for an emotionally bankrupt marriage. End the cold season by inviting the warmth of laughter into your home.

8. Laughter aids us through medical treatments and recovery. It may not cure cancer or heal a failing organ, but it can help you emotionally through the treatments and recovery. Norman Cousins states, "Laughter serves as a blocking agent. Like a bulletproof vest, it may help protect you against the ravages of negative emotions that can assault you in disease."[6]

9. Humor helps us cope. My all-time favorite quote on humor, attributed to nineteenth-century preacher Henry Ward Beecher, is, "A person without a sense of humor is like a wagon without springs, jolted by every pebble in the road. Good humor makes all things tolerable."[7] We don't always have a lot of say in the troubles and pressures that hit us, but we have everything to say about how we respond. Amy and I choose a marriage wagon with springs.

10. Laughter improves your overall attitude about yourself and the world around you. Remember when we used to watch the news to get information about what was going on in the world? Now we watch the news in the morning to see what we should be outraged about the rest of the day. I choose to watch the news, shake my head, and say, "God,

You've got this." Political pundits and politicians make me laugh. Try more laughter and less anger to make it through the day.

11. Laughter costs you nothing. Why is this an emotional benefit? Because I'm always happy when I get something for free. Laughter requires no special classes, equipment, or clothing.

12. Healthy laughter makes you more optimistic. Jabbing, cutting, sarcastic, and belittling humor moves us toward pessimism. Healthy humor paints a bright picture of a special future. A person with a sense of humor comes across as more positive.

13. Laughter decreases aggression. It is hard to be frustrated at a situation when you can find the humor in it. Amy and I know it better serves us to lighten up and laugh at bad customer service moments or on long delays at airports. I've never seen an act of aggression get anyone through TSA more quickly, make a plane take off faster, or help someone find a lost bag. Never happens. You might as well roll with it.

14. Laughter dispels bitterness, resentment, and anger. It is hard to stay mad at someone you laugh with. On your next date night, avoid sensitive topics or hot-button issues and cut loose. Enjoy one another and let your emotions level out.

The Physical Benefits of Laughter

15. Laughter turns your brain off. If you are prone to losing sleep because you can't turn your brain off, Amy and I know how you feel. Our minds race with lists, schedules, and agenda items when our heads hit the pillow. I fall asleep before Amy ninety-nine out of one hundred times. Her mind has a difficult time shutting off. Laughter forces us to think about other stuff. It frees the mind and in a sense shuts it down for a period of time.

Laugh enough and you won't need sleeping pills. The sleeping pill commercials on television terrify me. They offer a peaceful night's sleep with the possible side effects of aggressiveness, confusion, agitation, and hallucinations. Night night. Sweet dreams. Yes, you will sleep, but you'll have nightmares all night long. No thanks.

Laughter is a medicine that doesn't come in pill form, but offers unlimited doses for you and your marriage. You can take it anytime, anywhere, and it is absolutely free. There are no negative side effects to appropriate humor, and you don't need a doctor's prescription or a visit to the pharmacy.

If you indulge yourself with laughter during the day, you will sleep better at night. While there are other factors that affect sleep such as caffeine, loud neighbors, and late-night Taco Bell runs, there is plenty of research that proves hearty laughter aids in easing tension, turning off your brain, and giving you peace of mind.

16. When we laugh, we breathe in oxygen-rich air. Ever hear someone say, "Take a deep breath"? That's another way of saying, "Chill out, relax, it will be okay." Laughter is a deep breath, figuratively and literally. When you laugh, your rib cage expands and contracts more rapidly than it does when you breathe or talk.[8] If you've ever felt out of breath after a spell of laughing, now you know why.

17. Laughing burns calories. According to a Vanderbilt University study, you can shed up to forty calories a day with ten to fifteen minutes of laughter.[9] I wish my watch kept track of laughs alongside calories and steps. Laughter gives major organs, like the heart and lungs, a workout. I love walking out of a comedy movie feeling as though I got a workout.

18. Laughter reduces tension throughout your entire body. You know that relaxed feeling you get after exerting yourself in exercise? The same happens after you exert yourself in laughter. When you laugh, let it be strenuous. I love when people leave a date-night comedy show saying, "My face hurts" or "My side hurts." A hurting face or side is a good sign that you released a whole lot of tension.

19. Laughter relieves pain. The medical community understands the benefits of laughter and they have creative ways to use humor to help patients. Laughter therapy, also known as humor therapy, is part of the prescription to treat the whole patient—body and soul. Reputable hospitals and treatment centers such as Cancer Treatment Centers of America (CTCA) and Mayo Clinic are using laughter to help patients better cope as they receive conventional cancer treatments such as chemotherapy and radiation.

Laughter therapy sessions include circles of patients fake laughing. With their hands and fingers on their stomach, chest, or face, patients force laughter. Because laughter is contagious, watching others laugh leads them to follow suit.

Your mind can tell the difference between fake and real laughter, but your body can't. That means that our body reaps the physical benefits of fake laughter. According to cognitive neuroscientist Sophie Scott, all of the physical benefits of laughter are true for laughter that is helpless or forced.[10] This is very important for your marriage because it pushes us to laugh at our spouse's attempt at humor even if it is not funny. Don't waste the attempt. Fake laugh and let your body reap the benefits.

20. Laughter boosts the immune system and protects against disease. Studies out of Harvard Medical School show that laughter may help in the prevention of disease. They believe the boost in our immune systems is the result of increased activity among cells and antibodies, and improved blood flow throughout the entire body.[11]

21. Laughter lingers in marriage. Laughter allows us to capture a moment and carry it with us. When something strikes

Amy and me as funny, we anticipate laughing about it for years to come. We recently stayed at a high-end, posh hotel in New York City. I used Marriott points to get the room for free. It was one of those hotels that made us feel so welcome even though it felt like we didn't belong.

That night, I encouraged Amy to splurge and help herself to a snack from the mini bar. She chose a can of soda, without looking at the price sheet. On her third sip, I told her to slow down because each sip was about a dollar. It was then that I told her that her can of Diet Coke cost $8.00. Remember, laughter begins with shock. In this case she had the shock, but no immediate laughter. I'd say her shock led straight to frustration. She felt duped by the hotel.

We laughed for weeks following the most expensive soda of our married life. When a restaurant charges $3.50 for a soda or the movie theater $4.00, our callback is, "What a deal!"

When she's feeling bad about a Target receipt, I remind her, "Remember the time we spent $12.48 on a Diet Coke after tax and service charge?" No telling how many years that laugh will linger.

22. Laughter redeems bad moments you share as a couple.

On that same trip to New York City, we took in a Broadway show. It was not our cup of tea. Surrounded by show enthusiasts who loved it, we sat on the edge of our seats hoping it would get better. It never did. We've been to some great Broadway shows, but this one was slow-moving and the music did not connect with our souls.

At dinner that night, we both agreed that the more we talk about the show the worse it gets. The show cost a lot more than that Diet Coke. Now whenever I sing a line or two of a song I remember from the show, we laugh. It wasn't a great experience in the moment, but we've made our shared memory of it something to laugh about.

23. Laughter leads us to ask questions for deeper understanding. When you hear your spouse laugh in the other room, you immediately want to know what you missed. We want to understand where the laughter is coming from and why our spouse is laughing. It can be forced laughter, polite social laughter, or helpless laughter when we get caught up in the moment. Whatever the case, laughter requires that we investigate for deeper meaning. Laughter leads us to ask questions like "What did I miss?" "What's so funny?" "What happened?"

24. Laughter humanizes us. It's impossible to place yourself on a pedestal when laughing at yourself. Poking fun at yourself makes you more relatable. It leads others to think, "Yep, she's real." When you do or say something dumb, beat your spouse to the recognition of that fact. Laughter is a shake of the head acknowledging, "I can't believe I did that."

25. Laughter identifies couple friends. Finding friends where both the husbands and wives get along is challenging. When you find such couples, hold on to them. Amy and I have a few couple friends that we roar with every time we are together. Laughter discovers common ground and areas where our marriages overlap. "Yeah, that happened to us too" is a fast way to grow a friendship with another couple.

26. Laughter transcends all cultures. We may not be able to tell jokes in the same language, but we all laugh in the same language. Humor brings down walls and bonds us to those from different backgrounds, cultures, and denominations. Russian comedian and Branson, Missouri, entertainer Yakov Smirnoff once said, "Everybody laughs the same in every language because laughter is a universal connection."[12]

27. Fun and laughter extend time spent with those we love. Laughter is never in a rush to get away. It tugs at us to stay a bit longer, especially if we need to get back to work or other heavy responsibilities.

28. Laughter makes getting to know someone take less time. Familiarity is key in comedy. Carol Burnett taught fellow comedians that all comedy must start on the basis of familiarity. Research shows we find jokes told by famous comedians to be funnier than the same jokes told by someone we don't know.[13] Humor identifies similarities and downplays differences in short order.

29. Laughter makes you more attractive. If you've ever thought attractive people are more successful at work, you're not entirely wrong. But looks aren't everything. People who love to laugh exude a special presence that makes people want to gather around them. This is why so many singles list "sense of humor" on their list of qualities they look for in a potential mate.

The Spiritual Benefits of Laughter

30. Laughter sweetens faith, prayer, and sleep. Amy and I pray together before we kiss goodnight. And we also take to heart Reinhold Niebuhr's words: "Humor is a prelude to faith and laughter is the beginning of prayer."[14] My goal, after prayer, is to make Amy laugh at least once before we sleep. Enjoying one another and praying together gives us a good night's sleep.

31. Laughter pleases God. Did Jesus laugh? Do you think the sound of Jesus laughing pleased His Father in heaven? Author and joy advocate Randy Alcorn says, "Laughter is not only human, it's explicitly biblical and pleasing to God. It's therefore inconceivable to think that Jesus didn't laugh!"[15]

32. Laughter reminds us that we are image-bearers of God. We are created in the image of God, and our sense of humor is part of that image of God in man. In his book *50 Days of Heaven*, Randy Alcorn says:

> In Heaven, I believe our joy will often erupt in laughter. When laughter is prompted by what's appropriate, God always takes pleasure in it. I

think Christ will laugh with us, and his wit and fun-loving nature will be our greatest sources of endless laughter. Where did humor originate? Not with people, angels, or Satan. God created all good things, including good humor. If God didn't have a sense of humor, human beings, as his image-bearers wouldn't either. . . . God made us to laugh and to love to laugh.[16]

33. Laughter reveals joy. "The fruit of the Spirit is love, joy, peace, patience, kindness, goodness, faithfulness, gentleness [and] self-control" (Galatians 5:22-23). Laughter is an expression of joy. The fruit of the Spirit is different from the gifts of the Spirit. The gifts of the Spirit are distributed in varying combinations among believers. But all of the fruit of the Spirit is to be in all believers. Joy marks the life of maturing believers. That's why Psalm 100:1 invites us to "make a joyful noise to the LORD" and Philippians 4:4 implores us to "rejoice in the Lord always."

34. Laughter reminds us of the hope of heaven. I once heard a preacher say, "Don't be so heavenly minded that you're no earthly good." I thought that was strange considering how much we sang about heaven at church. When our thoughts are fixed on heaven it makes us more Kingdom minded on earth. When we laugh on earth, it is a picture of the laughter to come in heaven. Alcorn offers this thought for our consideration:

Jesus says, "Blessed are you who weep now, for you shall laugh" (Luke 6:21). In context, he's talking about people having great reward in Heaven. In other words, he's saying, "You will laugh in Heaven." Surely Jesus will join in the laughter—and be a source of much of it. And when Jesus laughs, it's always the laughter of both God and man.[17]

This upbeat hymn from my childhood is still one of my favorites:

> *When we all get to heaven,*
> *What a day of rejoicing that will be!*
> *When we all see Jesus,*
> *We'll sing and shout the victory.*[18]

One of the criticisms we receive at Woodland Hills Family Church is, "There are too many people and they laugh too much." One of our members, Mickey Pitman, has the perfect response, "If you don't like lots of people and laughter, then you won't like heaven either."

Martin Luther emphatically stated, "If they don't allow laughter in heaven then I don't want to go there. If the earth is fit for laughter then surely heaven is filled with it. Heaven is the birthplace of laughter."[19]

35. Humor opens us up for truth. Rabbi Sydney Mintz says, "When you laugh, aside from the endorphin rush, there's also a spiritual opening. You're not so tight inside yourself. That opening I've found to be a real gift, in people being able to absorb spirituality."[20]

36. Laughter is part of fellowship, one of the five purposes of the church. It pleases our Father when we enjoy one another in fellowship. Laughing with other believers shows a lost world that we enjoy spending time together. Maybe this is why the first-century Christians ate together with "glad and generous hearts" (Acts 2:46) and Solomon challenges us to "eat your bread with joy" (Ecclesiastes 9:7). Food and laughter go together. Save a seat at your dinner table for humor.

My childhood church sent kids to camp for a week every summer. Camp was full of outdoor activities, new friends, games, competitions, and lots of yelling, singing, storytelling, and laughing. Most every kid came home fired up for the Lord.

The Sunday night following camp, our pastor asked for testimonies and invited each kid to the front to share their experience and excitement. Every testimony ended with the same, "I can't wait to go back next year."

My pastor ended by saying, "Now kids, make sure you don't lose your fire for the Lord."

At ten years old, I remember thinking, *Why can't church be more like camp? Fun! Exciting! Joyful! Camp songs! Laughter!* It never made sense to me that we had environments where we permitted fun and laughter and other environments where it was frowned upon.

37. Laughter humbles us. It keeps us from overestimating our accomplishments and the person we think we've become. Ethel Barrymore notes, "You grow up the day you have your first real laugh—at yourself."[21] Humility revels in humor. Laughing at one's self admits to the world, "I need help. I don't have it all together."

Pastor Mark Batterson believes "that the happiest, healthiest, and holiest people on the planet are the people who laugh at themselves the most."[22]

38. Laughter ministers to others. Humor serves others. Mark Twain once said, "The best way to cheer yourself is to try to cheer someone else up."[23]

I lost a friend and longtime church member the day Bob Copeland went to be with the Lord. Bob always refreshed me. He never shared strong opinions about organizational decisions at the church, or at least he never voiced them to me. He had doubts and lots of questions. Engaging Bob in theological discourse was always a highlight for me. We laughed a lot together.

His last days were no different. I visited him three times after he went on hospice. The first two times Bob's body was weak, but his mind was sharp. We told stories and howled with laughter. I once had to shut down the laughter and say, "Bob, stop! I am not going to be responsible for your heart giving out."

Bob slept on my last visit. He lay in bed, on his side. His wife and daughter gathered around his bed with me, and I held his hand and prayed one final time. Many pauses filled the prayer as my emotions got the best of me. Bob ministered to me in that moment.

After our good-bye, he went to be with the Lord about an hour later. Bob entered the presence of the Lord and experienced a joy that overflows with singing, praise, rejoicing, and yes, laughter. Bob and I ministered to each other through humor often. He knew just when I needed a good laugh to work through a difficult or challenging time.

Laughter Has Limits

With all of the great benefits of laughter there is also a caution. We have so much to gain through humor and laughing, but there's a time, place, and purpose for it. Humor and laughter helped form a friendship between Bob and me, but there was a far greater purpose to our friendship, as well as his life, marriage, and family.

Ecclesiastes 7:1-4 teaches us how sorrow and humor, mourning and joy, sadness and laughter all work together:

A good name is better than precious ointment,
    and the day of death than the day of birth.
It is better to go to the house of mourning
    than to go to the house of feasting,
for this is the end of all mankind,
    and the living will lay it to heart.
Sorrow is better than laughter,

for by sadness of face the heart is made glad.
The heart of the wise is in the house of mourning,
but the heart of fools is in the house of mirth.

Why is it better to go to a funeral (the house of mourning) than to a party (the house of feasting)? It's better because you don't leave a party or comedy club saying, "I will never be the same after that." That's what you say when you leave a funeral, or at least what you should say. Funerals are recalibrating events because "the heart of the wise is in the house of mourning." The wise person sits at a funeral and asks him- or herself a host of questions:

How am I loving my family?

What do I need to change?

Am I wasting my life?

Will anyone show up at my funeral?

Sometimes the aging members of our congregation tell me, "I don't want a funeral. Bury me and have a party." I sometimes wonder if that dismissive request comes from the one who fears that no one will show up. That was actually one of Bob's fears, but a packed chapel proved otherwise.

A funeral shares the highlight reel of one's life. We focus on good times and deeds while downplaying struggles, habits, and hang-ups. Family and friends eulogize their lost loved one with words of high value. I often think to myself, *I sure hope they didn't wait until now to share these words. I trust they took the time to say them while he (she) was with them.* The regret one feels at a funeral is steeped in the thought, *I wish I had said . . .*

My kids give me a hard time for how often I talk about my funeral. I guess when you're a pastor, it comes with the territory. I want my funeral to be celebratory, yes, but I also want people to leave challenged to be better spouses and parents. When Solomon says, "Sorrow is better than laughter" (Ecclesiastes 7:3), he clearly defines the limits of laughter. Sorrow leads us to ask probing questions.

The Refreshment of Laughter

Laughter-filled parties offer us relief from the grind of life and bond us with others. The house of mourning goes straight to the heart and forces a decision. Will I change my life, marriage, family, speech, and pursuit of career based on taking to heart the death of my loved one? Don't rush out of mourning until you have soaked up every possible lesson. This brings you something that laughter does not.

The church I grew up in had a singing evangelist family visit almost every year. It was grandma, grandpa, their son, and his family on a bus. They were my favorite family to have visit because they were all down-to-earth people. They preached what they believed and lived what they preached. Grandpa was a strong fundamentalist preacher who shouted with the best of them. His sermons were strong, loud, and convicting.

I don't remember any of his sermons, but I do remember one illustration he used that set the tone for the rest of the messages I heard him preach. He told the story of a conversation he had with a man at a church he regularly visited.

In the middle of a weeklong revival, the man approached the evangelist and said, "Preacher, please go easy on us tonight. It's been a long week and I already feel pretty beat up." His tone was gracious and polite, but it struck a nerve in the preacher. I believe the Lord brought some balance to the tone and message of that old-time religion, circuit-riding, hellfire-and-brimstone minister. He received the man's request.

Laughter is a break from the grind of life, even for the most serious Christian.

Your Laughter Score

For a possible 20,000 points,

1. Laugh Therapy. Stand two to three feet away from your spouse, place your fingertips on your jaw, and belly laugh with several hearty "he-he-he-he-hes," "ho-ho-ho-ho-hos," and "ha-ha-ha-ha-has." Repeat with your hands on your stomach. Continue until you get a reaction from your spouse. This may take two to three minutes.

My attempt at humor . . .

Fell flat...0 points

Made my spouse smirk..............................1,000 points

Made my spouse smile................................2,000 points

Made my spouse snicker.............................3,000 points

Made my spouse giggle ....4,000 points

Made my spouse chuckle............................5,000 points

Made my spouse cackle ....6,000 points

Made my spouse belly laugh.......................7,000 points

Made my spouse howl.................................8,000 points

Made my spouse shriek ....9,000 points

Made my spouse die laughing................... 10,000 points

_____ Her Score _____ His Score

The next time I attempt this humor, I will

_____

2. Tickle Yourself and Each Other. Start by tickling yourself. You'll notice it doesn't work. You can't make yourself laugh by tickling. Now invite your spouse to tickle you. The more you open yourself up for laughter, the more contagious it will be for your spouse. In other words, your score depends completely on your willingness to let go and let it happen.

My attempt at humor . . .

Fell flat .... 0 points
Made my spouse smirk .... 1,000 points
Made my spouse smile .... 2,000 points
Made my spouse snicker .... 3,000 points
Made my spouse giggle .... 4,000 points
Made my spouse chuckle .... 5,000 points
Made my spouse cackle .... 6,000 points
Made my spouse belly laugh .... 7,000 points
Made my spouse howl .... 8,000 points
Made my spouse shriek .... 9,000 points
Made my spouse die laughing .... 10,000 points

_____ Her Score _____ His Score

The next time I attempt this humor, I will

_____

Write your scores on page 205, too.

Conversation Starters and a Few More Laughs

- Which benefits of laughter surprised you?

- Are there any benefits of laughter you would add to this list?

- When was the last time you laughed at a funeral and why?

- What funny story do you want your family to share about you at your funeral?

- What lesson will people "take to heart" at your funeral?

CHAPTER 3

You're Funnier than You Think

Studying humor is like dissecting a frog.
You might learn a lot about it, but
you wind up with a dead frog.

E. B. WHITE

———————

From there to here, from here to there,
funny things are everywhere.

DR. SEUSS

"I'M NOT FUNNY."

"People get bored with my stories."

"I can deliver the premise of a joke, but always forget the punch line."

"My spouse is the funny one."

"I take life too seriously."

"I have a dry sense of humor that my spouse doesn't appreciate."

When prompted by these thoughts, do you avoid attempts at humor? People often tell me, "Laughter is easy in your marriage because you're funny. I'm not funny." Here are two terms for you:

In the Hebrew, "Hogwash."

In the Greek, "Baloney!"

"I'm not funny" is no excuse! The potential for humor is in all of us. You just need to dig a little.

I recently encountered a man in a church service who sat on the front row with a stone-cold expression on his face. He expressed zero emotion while the crowd around him roared with laughter. Toward the end of the message something struck him as funny and he smiled. That was enough to remind me that those who laugh little, still laugh. Humor is in all of us. Like our personalities, we have different senses of humor. We need to tap into them.

There are some low-entry factors and skills to help you discover your marital funny bone together. Age, personality, and years married bear no weight in getting better at humor. Let's explore some ways to help you grow in humor.

1. Look for Funny Rather than Trying to Be Funny

The first and easiest entry into humor is observational. Open your eyes. Humor is everywhere.

I shared this with my senior adult friend and longtime member of Woodland Hills Family Church, Pat Kershaw, over coffee one morning at Panera Bread. I asked her if she had seen something funny lately. Of all places, she found something funny at the Catholic hospital in Springfield, Missouri, and let out a good chuckle.

Bible verses line the hallways of this hospital. On the wall in the room where she received a mammogram, the verse read, "We are hard pressed on every side, but not crushed" (2 Corinthians 4:8, NIV). With that, I almost spat my hazelnut blend across the table. I don't know who selected that verse, but I'm assuming it was a nun with a great sense of humor. The verse out of context is funny, but hearing it from an eighty-four-year-old member of your church is funnier. She shared it with a bashfulness that suggested she thought she was telling me a dirty joke. I assured her she was not.

Observational humor requires the skill of awareness. It focuses our minds to look at ordinary, mundane, and at times frustrating and exhausting moments in brand-new ways. Like seeing a simple sign at a public pool that reads, "Swimsuits required." Let your mind run with it. What happened that caused someone to display that sign? Did someone stand on the side of a crowded pool and say, "I'm tired of the constraints society places on me. Yes, everyone in here is wearing a bathing suit, but today no one will tell *me* what to do."

On walks with Amy, I look for funny. Recently we saw a sign displaying a city ordinance that I know must have been demanded by a hovering parent:

Dog Waste
Is a Threat to the
Health of Our Children,
Degrades Our Town,
and Transmits Disease.
Clean Up after
Your Pet.
Ord. #2.5.220

What helicopter parent stood up at a city hall meeting and petitioned for that ordinance and sign? Did the aldermen keep a straight face? Or did one stand up and say in protest, "How will our kids ever learn to clean poop off of their shoes with a little twig, or scrape it off on the sidewalk, then brush the remnant off in the grass?" Amy and I got several laughs off of that one sign.

We all step in manure, literally and figuratively. Instead of creating environments for our children to be perfectly safe and free from excrement, let's teach them how to be safe in environments they can't control. Teach them how to watch their steps. But also teach them to laugh and not go to pieces when they do "step in it."

Unusual signs or odd behavior in others give us plenty of material to work with on a daily basis. Peter McGraw calls these disruptions to our thinking "violations." They disrupt how we think things ought to be. But our reactions to these violations can go in different directions.

McGraw is a professor at the University of Colorado Boulder, the founder of the Humor Research Lab (HuRL), and the author of *The Humor Code*. He has a fun job researching what makes things funny. He believes that humor is pervasive and beneficial, and influences our choices. He runs HuRL with his colleague Caleb Warren, and together they developed the Benign Violation Theory (BVT). We laugh when our brain is shocked, yes, but the Benign Violation Theory explains the difference between being shocked and laughing and being shocked and angry.[1]

A violation is "anything that threatens the way you believe the world ought to be." It's a trigger in your brain that says, "Something seems wrong. That does not fit with the way I perceive the world." The primary example he uses is someone falling down. We laugh when a person falls and is uninjured, but we don't laugh if they are hurt. If we laugh at someone who is hurt, that is maligned humor and not healthy. The fact that the person shakes it off makes it benign.

Comedian Jason Earls does a bit in his set called "Smoking in Church." With a fake cigarette in his mouth, he requests a bulletin from an usher, sings *This Is the Air I Breathe*, and even "Amens" the preacher. We laugh because no one would ever think to smoke in a church service. It is a fantastic violation that is benign because it is a gentle and acceptable joke, since the chances of it ever happening are next to zilch.

Church signs provide a lot of material for laughter:

Our church is like a Snickers, sweet with a few nuts.

Whoever stole our church AC units, keep one because it's hot where you're going.

Church signs are not the only places where Christians' goofiness is on display. You observe plenty of humor in church bulletins, too:

The pastor will preach his farewell message, after which the choir will sing, "Break Forth into Joy."

The rosebud on the altar this morning is to announce the birth of David Alan Belzer, the sin of Reverend and Mrs. Julius Belzer.

Remember in prayer the many who are sick of our church and community.

At the evening service tonight, the sermon topic will be "What Is Hell?" Come early and listen to our choir practice.

Today's Sermon: "How Much Can a Man Drink?" with hymns from a full choir.

Tuesday at 4 p.m. there will be an ice cream social. All ladies giving milk will please come early.

Weight Watchers will meet at 7 p.m. Please use large double door at the side entrance.

The Ladies Bible Study will be held Thursday morning at 10. All ladies are invited to lunch in the fellowship hall after the B.S. is done.

Ladies, don't forget the rummage sale. It's a chance to get rid of those things not worth keeping around the house. Don't forget your husbands.

The ladies of the church have cast off clothing of every kind. They may be seen in the basement on Friday.

Pastor is on vacation. Massages can be given to church secretary.

What violations are passing you by? Over dinner, ask your spouse, "Did you see anything funny today?" On your next date night, errand, or ride to church, spend some time watching people. Not for the purpose of making fun of them, but for the opportunity to see some of the craziness that lies in all of us. Observe more and you will laugh more.

2. Lean Into Your Spouse's Sense of Humor to Create Your Shared Sense of Humor

My wife wants you to know that she is not a comedian. I wrote this chapter with her in mind. She hates telling jokes because she has a core fear of forgetting the punch line. In twenty-three years of marriage, I can probably count on one hand the number of times she's told a joke to me, our kids, family, or friends. The thought of telling a joke or funny story makes her break out in a cold sweat. When all eyes are on her, she throws up a little bit in the back of her mouth.

A few times in recent years, she's launched into the premise of a joke in which everyone responded with open mouths and wide eyes as if to say, "Yay, Amy! You got this! Go for it!" only for her to quit in the middle of the joke and walk away. We chase after her screaming, "You can't leave us hanging!" The torture of it all gives us big laughs. She's good. She knows how to leave us wanting more.

My wife has so much confidence in everything she does, except this one area. "I save that for you," she tells me. "This marriage doesn't need two comedians." But the fact is, we are two people who love to laugh and we constantly find humor in everything we do, everywhere we go, and with everyone we spend time with.

Laughter is part of attraction and chemistry, but finding a funny spouse is not the goal. You're not looking for a comedian; you're looking for someone who wants to grow with you. This growth includes developing your shared sense of humor. If your spouse can't tell funny jokes, no biggie. Marital satisfaction does not hinge on one's ability to crack a joke.

Jeffrey Hall, researcher at the University of Kansas, looked at the findings of thirty-nine studies with over 15,000 participants over the last thirty years to better understand the importance of humor in relationships. "That people think you are funny or you can make a joke out of anything is not strongly related to relationship satisfaction. What is strongly related to relationship satisfaction is the humor that couples create together." He added, "It's not about being a great comedian, but finding what's funny in the everyday and enjoying it together."[2]

There are several ways Amy and I have developed our shared sense of humor over the years. First, we ask each other a lot of questions for greater understanding. When she laughs at something and I don't, I ask, "What did I miss?" Often she is giving me another side or perspective that I didn't see. When I see it through her eyes, I can laugh with her.

Second, we bump knees under the table while eating with friends and family. When something awkward happens, our shared sense of humor kicks in. And like Morse code, we start bumping knees under the table as a way of saying, "Can you believe this is happening right now?" Amy also uses the under-the-table code to restrain me and my mouth. She knows what's about to come out of my mouth, and her gentle nudge keeps me out of trouble.

Third, our shared sense of humor is built off of our shared history together. The longer you are married, the greater your shared sense of humor should be. This is simple but practical. Give your marriage time. You need shared experiences from events such as vacations, church services, road trips, holidays, meals, phone calls, meetings, work parties, birthday parties, and children to develop your shared sense of humor.

Finding funny in everyday life requires a shared sense of

humor that strikes a balance between serious and silly. Life can't be serious all the time just as it can't be one big joke. We all know people who never crack a smile and have little to no joy in their homes. We also know those who never take anything seriously. Each of these extremes is unhealthy. We want our serious friends to lighten up at times, and we want our joking friends to be able to enter into deeper, contemplative moments.

Our shared sense of humor helps us achieve this balance between serious and lighthearted. Humor compatibility is more than a couple's ability to make each other laugh. It goes deeper than that. It gives us the ability to move through difficult moments and challenging circumstances with an appropriate level of lightheartedness. Because we know each other so well after twenty-three years of marriage, our shared sense of humor helps guide us through life's most challenging and even embarrassing moments.

What is your most embarrassing moment ever?

Amy and I, along with every one of you who attended high school, share the gut-wrenching moment when we saw a kid trip and dump a tray of food. We both agree that if that had happened to us, we would have transferred schools immediately.

Having an unzipped fly while preaching ranks high on the list too. For Amy, public speaking alone is at the top of her list.

The most embarrassing moment of my life came on a plane during the summer of 2016.

I struggle with vasovagal syncope. It is a condition that causes me to pass out for a few minutes at a time. My body shuts down when triggered by stress, anxiety, the sight of blood, or human suffering. When my fatigue combines with another's suffering, I am out cold for fifteen to thirty minutes. My heart rate and blood pressure plummet suddenly, causing reduced blood flow to the brain. Avoiding the triggers is the only remedy I have against losing consciousness.

I passed out when my coworker in college drove a piece of rebar through his hand. I threw his arm over my shoulder and rushed him to the nurse's station. When the nurse saw us, she asked, "Who's hurt?" My friend and I both were on the verge of passing out. We were white as ghosts.

I passed out in 1996 on my first pastoral hospital visit. I had driven all through the night to start my new job as an associate pastor, running on just two hours of sleep. The senior pastor drove me to the hospital to visit a woman who had miscarried. Standing by her bedside listening to the doctor talk to the woman, my vasovagal kicked in. Next thing I remember, I was prostrate in the hall with a nurse standing over me offering me cookies and juice.

I passed out when my daughter cut her upper lip while searching for lizards at a state park. Then I passed out again a few hours later after leaving the emergency room when she pulled the fresh stitches out of her still-numb lip. We were on a bridge when I started to go out that time.

I fainted after leading the senior class at Liberty University in a graduate's pledge at our commencement. No human suffering that time, other than finals. I was so exhausted my body shut down and I was toast.

If I pass out while with strangers, my last words are, "Don't call an ambulance." I go out for fifteen to thirty minutes and wake up energized and in need of a light snack. Peanut butter on crackers is my craving.

The older I get, the worse my vasovagal syncope gets. The following story almost didn't make this book. We wrestled with sharing it for many reasons, but I believe full disclosure helps me deal with it. We can laugh about it now, and the funny thing is, we laughed about it the day it happened. Again, the older we get the less seriously we take ourselves.

Amy and I dropped off our kids, Corynn and Carson, at church to catch the bus for a week at summer camp in Florida. The next day, we boarded a plane for Mexico and our long-anticipated annual abandon. We had books to read and movies to watch. It was our week. No pressure. No anxiety. No fatigue.

My assigned seat was 8E, a center seat. Amy took 8F at the window.

About an hour after takeoff, Amy pressed Play on a movie that would soon take me out. *The Impossible*, rated PG-13, is about the tragic tsunami that hit Thailand in December 2004. Thirty minutes into the movie, my triggers went off. The human suffering in that movie was too much for me.

I looked over at Amy and she saw the color leave my face and the rings form under my eyes. At this point, we knew we had sixty to ninety seconds to prepare the environment, and those around us, for my brief period of rest. The guy in 8D was asleep, so we didn't inform him. We immediately cleared the tray tables of sodas and snacks, and I leaned over into Amy's lap and went out.

When I came to, I asked, "How long was I out?"

Amy answered, "About twenty minutes."

There was silence mixed with shock. Before I passed out, I had been well hydrated. But when I woke up, my seat was well hydrated. Never in a million years did I plan on passing out on this flight. Come on! We were on vacation! I was totally rested and without a worry in the world.

"Amy?" I asked in shock as I looked down at my soaked seat. "Why didn't you wake me?"

"I had no idea," she reassured me. "Besides, I was too busy taking your pulse and making sure you were still breathing."

We were an hour from landing and I was in full crisis mode. I grabbed everything out of my carry-on that would absorb this mess and went to work, saving my pullover fleece to wrap around my waist. I asked the flight attendant for some napkins and did a pretty good job of cleanup. Then I gave Amy some instructions for how it would go down at the gate and terminal.

"When we hit the gate and the seatbelt sign goes off, let's remain in our seats. When our row empties, I'll grab my bag and we'll head straight to baggage claim. Once we get our bags, I'll head straight to the bathroom and this whole ordeal will be behind us," I explained. Amy agreed.

Taxiing to the gate took forever. We had a plan, but we did not think of everything.

About ten seconds after the seatbelt sign went off, I heard the lady in the seat behind me say to her husband, "My purse is soaked!"

Fear and trembling hit me so fast and hard I asked the Lord to make me pass out again. I would rather have gotten taken off the plane on a stretcher than explain to the lady what happened.

I didn't have time to react because their conversation escalated.

As she started drying off some of her makeup brushes and accessories, her husband was trying to figure it out: "There must be an air conditioning leak or something."

"Honey, this is a lot of water for an air conditioning drip," she said as she shook off one of her lipsticks. Amy and I were speechless and gripped with shock.

We raced off the plane, I changed in the bathroom, we drove to the hotel and thought we were in the clear. We took all soiled items, including my carry-on bag, straight to the resort's laundry room and put it in one load.

That night at dinner, feeling like a total man, I flexed my muscles for Amy and said, "You lucked out with me, babe." As we laughed, the couple from seats 9E and 9F walked into the restaurant. At this point I had two options. Should I buy their meal anonymously and avoid them like the plague the rest of the week or come clean? I won't tell you what we did. That's between us and the Lord.

Talk about a callback. This is a biggie for us. This story will go with me for the rest of my life.

My son is following in my comedic footsteps and loves the callback of this story. When he is with me on a flight, he likes to look in the row behind us and say, "Ma'am, you might want to put your bag in the overhead bin." He will have that callback until the Lord calls me home.

3. Make Attempts, Fail, and Keep Trying

I love chili. It's my favorite leftover meal. When Amy makes it on Monday, we have it all week. It gets better as the week goes along. By Wednesday it is fantastic. Comedy and joke-telling work the exact same way. Give it time to meld together.

Think of your favorite comedian. Got someone in mind? The reason the comedian's routine makes you laugh so hard is that you're hearing the jokes for the first time, but it isn't the first time the comedian shared the material. The comedian delivered that joke hundreds of times before recording it. Audience participation, feedback, timing, gestures, and editing were added over time. Your marriage laughter score will get better the more attempts you make, and the more you practice.

So what are you waiting for? Tell your spouse some jokes. Look up a few online and share them over dinner.

Recount a story from your day and add some physical humor to it. Dance. Fall on the floor. Exaggerate your facial expressions. Use melodramatic hand gestures.

Mix up your laugh style. You're not required to stick with the same laugh you've had your whole life. Try a new one. We love Tripp and Tyler's Laughing Styles video, where they categorize laughs like the Chuckle, the Wheezer, the Clapper, the Machine Gun, the Cackler, the Joke Repeater, the Donald Duck, the High Society, the Lost Control, the Mimer, the Whiplasher, All Nostrils, the Baby Waker, and the Splatterer.[3]

We've created some of our own definitions. I have a "raspy slow machine-gun" laugh. Amy has a "silent, patriotic" laugh. I call it patriotic because she always places her hand over her heart so as to hold in the laughter. I tell her, "Like a sneeze, it's dangerous to hold it in. You've got to let it out." Have your spouse call out a laugh style and you impersonate it. Name a member of the family and attempt their laugh style. The next time your spouse says or does something funny, use a laugh style that is outside the box.

The green room of a comedy show, where multiple comedians are gathered, is like a think tank. "I'm trying new stuff out tonight." "You know what you should add to that new bit?" "Have you ever thought about doing a bit on mammograms?" That's the shop talk of stand-ups. Comedians are constantly working on material. Benevolent veterans love to help the rookies, and wise rookies soak it up.

Andrew Tarvin, an engineer turned stand-up comedian, travels the globe teaching companies how humor makes the workplace more creative, productive, and profitable. He teaches people the skill of humor.[4] Did you catch that? Humor is a skill, which means you can learn it. Through practice and repetition, we can get better at it. For those of you who say, "I'm not funny," you need to start trying. Don't give up after a few failed attempts. Keep working at it and ask for input.

For example, I'm not a magician, but I do know a few tricks. I can make a coin disappear and magically reappear from behind your ear. With more practice, I could learn more tricks and perfect the ones I already know.

I'm not a chef, and my knife skills in the kitchen look nothing like what you see on Food Network's *Iron Chef.* But if I spent hours in the kitchen this week, I would get better.

I had a shot at being one of the greatest athletes of the twentieth century, but I lack balance, strength, coordination, and skill. One summer while my friends played baseball up the street, I learned how to juggle. I was eight, had some time on my hands, and a fresh can of Penn tennis balls that my Grandma Mary Jane gave me.

The first day, I dropped the balls on every attempt. By day two, I succeeded with a few rotations before dropping one. Day three brought great confidence and a few minutes without a drop. Day four came with audience participation, when I had my brother throw me a ball to get started. By the end of the week, I was ready for my first performance. In the weeks that followed, I juggled fruit, tennis rackets, tools, and towels. Almost forty years later, I've still got it. Not professional level, but the skill stuck.

Don't sell yourself short. Commit to the performance. Practice in front of a mirror, in the shower, or while driving. My family often catches me "talking to myself," but I'm just practicing.

Humor is risky. Not every attempt to make your spouse laugh succeeds. Like a comedian who cuts a flat bit from his or her set, so shall I. When your attempt at humor falls flat, be okay with it. Go with it. To paraphrase Winston Churchill, success in humor is moving from one flat joke to another with undiminished enthusiasm.

4. Turn Up Appropriate Humor and Mute Inappropriate Humor

This is the most important caution of the book. When I told family and friends about this book, the number one comment I received was, "Make sure you teach spouses how to laugh with, not at, each other." This is great feedback and seems to be a concern for many.

Laughing at yourself and with your spouse is appropriate. It can be healing, playful, kind, uplifting, encouraging, and life giving. If you initiate self-deprecating humor and invite your spouse to join you, make sure that it doesn't turn into making fun of your spouse. You may be in the mood for poking fun at yourself, but your spouse may not want to poke fun at him- or herself. In such a case, there's always the potential of hurting feelings.

Laughing at others is okay when the others are inviting you to do so, but don't cross the line. If you do, simply say, "I'm sorry, I took that too far."

Sometimes we say "laughing at others," when we really

mean "making fun of others." Making fun of another is always inappropriate, hurtful, and belittling.

Men tend to relate to one another using sarcasm and talking smack. One wife recently told me, "My husband's sarcasm doesn't play well in our marriage. I'm not one of the boys. After he spends time with friends, I get the high-school version of him at home. We may have met in high school, but I was kind of hoping he would grow out of it."

Understanding the different types of humor helps us create lines for what is appropriate and what is not. Psychology researcher Rod Martin categorized humor into four main styles:

1. Affiliative humor means cracking jokes, engaging in banter, and otherwise using humor to make others like us.

2. Self-enhancing humor is an optimistic, coping humor, characterized by the ability to laugh at yourself or at the absurdity of a situation and feel better as a result.

3. Aggressive humor is characterized by sarcasm, teasing, criticism, and ridicule.

4. Self-defeating humor is attempting to get others to like us by putting ourselves down.[5]

A healthy marriage matures in humor and leans into affiliative and self-enhancing humor and away from aggressive and self-defeating humor. In other words, don't be annoying, and know when you've gone too far. Confess and learn from your mistakes.

For example, I went too far on our honeymoon. We booked a snorkeling excursion in the Bahamas during a three-day cruise. We were two Midwesterners in love and poised for adventure. Fifty people joined us that afternoon as we selected our fins, masks, snorkels, and life vests out of fifty-five-gallon drums bungeed to a rickety old deck boat.

The captain told us to line up and jump off the back of the boat two at a time about ten seconds apart. While standing in the middle of the line, I put my gear on and Amy did not.

"What are you doing?" I asked.

She said, "I don't want to jump right in. I'm gonna sit on the edge of the boat and get my feet wet first, then I'll put on my gear." She likes to acclimate to the water.

Married for only two days, I had no idea how she would accomplish all of that in less than ten seconds. I didn't want to hold up the line, so I had my own plan.

Wouldn't it be funny if I pushed her in? I thought to myself. *She will laugh, find my playfulness cute, and we won't hold up the line.*

When the couple in front of us jumped in, I counted to ten, placed my arm around Amy, and we jumped. Or more accurately, I jumped and pulled Amy in with me.

I had no idea how hard it was to put all of this equipment on while in the water. She didn't smirk, smile, or snicker. Nope. She was flabbergasted and flat-out annoyed.

My attempt at humor went too far. I learned my lesson, and twenty-three years later we stay out of the ocean altogether.

5. Know the Time and Place for Humor

My friend Shane Stanford pastors Christ United Methodist Church in Memphis, Tennessee. It was a Friday night in Memphis. I arrived at the church with my daughter for a couples' comedy night. We set up the book table, ate dinner with the Stanfords, then prepared for the show.

The show had a simple format. Shane was supposed to give the welcome and introduction and I was supposed to bring the jokes. We didn't even make it out of the welcome and introduction before everything fell apart. I walked on stage, grabbed the microphone, and went in for the obligatory hug. A guy interrupted our hug and whispered in Shane's ear, "A man just entered the building with a shotgun."

My heart felt like it had stopped. I immediately jumped off the stage and headed to the lobby where my daughter sat at the book table. It was the longest ten-second jog of my life. As I hit the lobby and approached her, my dad tone came out. You know what the dad tone is, right? It's the tone that means business and your kids know it. Every dad has the tone.

"Corynn Mae, come here now!" The "now" was deep and authoritative. Also, throwing in the middle name gives it an extra pop. Corynn jumped up and came right over to me. I grabbed her by the arm and walked her down to the front row.

For fifteen minutes we didn't know what was going on. Shane asked that no one leave, but about twenty dads ignored his call. The children of the attendees were down a level and over in another part of the building. I have to assume that half of the dads were packing heat.

Thirty Memphis police officers responded to the scene. They swept the building and several entered our banquet room. Moms cried and the men looked ready for war. Few words were spoken.

Finally, head held down in relief, Shane walked to the front to make an announcement. The high school, which was adjacent to the church, had had a rehearsal that night for a play called *The Wild West*. A teenage actor, not really thinking, walked into the building with a fake double-barrel shotgun. Relieved, I looked out at sobbing moms wanting to go see their children. I stood with Shane as he prayed. After his prayer, dads started to return to the room. Hugs exchanged between spouses showed their relief.

I asked Shane, "What do you want to do?"

He said, "I think you should get started." Obviously he was in shock. No one was ready to hear me say, "A pastor, a priest, and rabbi walk into a . . ."

The crowd, timing, content, and delivery were all wrong. I wanted to cancel or postpone the event, but Shane lives by the motto, "The Show Must Go On!"

There is a right time and place for humor. The right time and place for humor in your marriage has more to do with your spouse than it does you. Your spouse may not be in the mood after a long day and just needs a few minutes to decompress. Content and delivery are important, but picking your moment is important too. Like a great quarterback who reads the defense, read your spouse's mood. You may need to hold the humor for a bit.

This is important for the callback. When something challenging happens and you want to make a joke, it may better serve you to make a mental note, give it some time, and bring it back up later. I learned this lesson the hard way as well.

My wife was in the kitchen making brussels sprouts salad for a gathering of friends. She diced, chopped, and tossed the most gorgeous bowl of greens a party has ever seen. It took her over an hour to prepare.

A few weeks earlier we had bought the coolest new lids made out of silicone and shaped like flowers and lily pads. When laid on top, the lid immediately suctions itself to the bowl and forms a seal. It's a remarkable invention. We tried it in the store a dozen times before deciding we had to have it.

When she finished making the salad, she laid the flower cover over the bowl. I saw her trying it again like we did in the store and her amazement was still there. She then picked up the salad by the lid, not the bowl, and walked over to the refrigerator. On the walk over, she looked at me and said, "This thing is amazing!"

No sooner did those words come out of her mouth, than the bowl detached from the lid and plummeted to the floor.

It all happened in slow motion. The bowl shattered and salad went everywhere. On the fridge, under the fridge, on the cabinets, and under the cabinets. Brussels sprouts touched every surface in the kitchen.

The timing shocked me. Had it happened without her saying anything, it wouldn't have been as funny. But the fact that she said, "This thing is amazing," right before it created the biggest disaster in the history of our kitchen, makes the whole scenario so memorable.

Right before I burst into laughter, Amy's heart sank. There were no tears, but she walked right over the mess and out of the kitchen. I interpreted that to mean, "Ted, you're cleaning this up." So I did.

Carson walked into the kitchen while I was on my knees picking sprout shreds out of the grout. "What happened?" he asked.

With a smirk, I said, "Come down here, you're never going to believe this one." I shared the story with him. He was in shock and saw the humor in the whole mess.

A few minutes later, Amy came back to the kitchen. "Ain't I doing an *amazing* job cleaning this kitchen?" I asked, emphasizing the word *amazing* with the same tone she had used. It was too soon.

"Too soon" is an expression we all use when we crack jokes before the recipient is ready to receive them.

I asked, "Too soon?" of our congregation after cracking jokes on the Sunday after the 2016 presidential election and again a year later after attempting humor over the NFL Take the Knee boycott. I asked it of Amy as well that day on bended knee in our kitchen. She needed more time.

Read your spouse and know when your new callback is ready for delivery. "This thing is amazing" is a fantastic callback for us. I use it almost daily with Amy as my witness. I love our blender and coffeepot. We've had them for years and they never let us down. I remind Amy often, "These appliances are amazing!"

Your Laughter Score

For a possible 20,000 points,

1. Disaster Recovery. Do you have a story of a disaster in your kitchen, mishap around the house, a dirty diaper that exploded, or a do-it-yourself project that went terribly wrong? What happened? Who cleaned it up? Did you laugh right away? How much time did you need before you found the funny in it? Have you told your kids, family, or friends? Take turns sharing a story of your favorite disaster.

My attempt at humor . . .

Fell flat...0 points
Made my spouse smirk.............................1,000 points
Made my spouse smile............................2,000 points

Made my spouse snicker .... 3,000 points

Made my spouse giggle .... 4,000 points

Made my spouse chuckle .... 5,000 points

Made my spouse cackle .... 6,000 points

Made my spouse belly laugh .... 7,000 points

Made my spouse howl .... 8,000 points

Made my spouse shriek .... 9,000 points

Made my spouse die laughing .... 10,000 points

_____ Her Score _____ His Score

The next time I attempt this humor, I will

_____

2. Physical Humor. Comedians like Jerry Lewis and Steve Martin are the best examples of this kind of comedy. Though statistics vary according to the study, some experts say that body language and facial expressions make up 55 percent of spoken communication, so it makes sense to throw your entire body into the story or joke. Don't just tell your spouse what happened at work or home today. Throw your whole body into it. Here are a few examples to get started using physical humor:

- Recount a story of a time you saw a child pitching a fit in a store.

- Demonstrate using an exercise machine you would feel uncomfortable on.

• What was the most embarrassing moment in your life? Recall an incident when you wanted to crawl into a hole and die. Act it out physically as you relive the details.

My attempt at humor . . .

Fell flat..0 points
Made my spouse smirk...............................1,000 points
Made my spouse smile................................2,000 points
Made my spouse snicker.............................3,000 points
Made my spouse giggle...............................4,000 points
Made my spouse chuckle............................5,000 points
Made my spouse cackle ....6,000 points
Made my spouse belly laugh.......................7,000 points
Made my spouse howl.................................8,000 points
Made my spouse shriek ....9,000 points
Made my spouse die laughing..................10,000 points

_____ Her Score _____ His Score

The next time I attempt this humor, I will

_____

Write your scores on page 206, too.

Conversation Starters and a Few More Laughs

- Which flower best describes your spouse first thing in the morning? Why?

     A. Morning Glory
     B. Bird of Paradise
     C. Snapdragon
     D. Sunflower

- On a scale of 1 to 10 (1 being "not too funny," 10 being "very funny"), how funny are you? How funny is your spouse?

- Did you see anything funny today?

- Is there any inappropriate humor in your marriage that needs to be eliminated?

CHAPTER 4

Coo, Coo, My Dove

If you wish to glimpse inside a human soul and get to know the man, don't bother analyzing his ways of being silent, of talking, of weeping, or seeing how much he is moved by noble ideas; you'll get better results if you just watch him laugh. If he laughs well, he's a good man. . . . All I claim to know is that laughter is the most reliable gauge of human nature.

FEODOR DOSTOYEVSKY

If one gives an answer before he hears, it is his folly and shame.

PROVERBS 18:13

THE SECRET TO great communication in marriage is connection, not information. Early in our marriage, I thought Amy wanted answers. I was wrong. Once I learned that communication was more than communicating facts and details about my day, I started to enjoy our conversations more, even the tough ones. Laughter turned what felt like business-meeting conversations and agendas into fun times of reconnection.

Amy thinks I'm an expert on everything. This tempts me to swell with pride, but it also places pressure on me to perform. When we watch movies, she asks questions about the movie that I have no idea how to answer. If the movie is about the CIA, she'll ask me detailed questions about espionage. If the setting of the movie is in space, I get asked about NASA. That she thinks I have answers to these complicated questions is a badge of honor.

When we were first married, driving through a construction zone spurred many questions. "What are they doing here?" "How many lanes are they putting in?" "When do you think this will be done?" I reminded her, "I wasn't involved in any of the meetings on this project." That's when I thought she wanted answers. When I came to the understanding that she wanted connection, not information, everything changed.

Now when she asks me questions in a construction zone, I turn into the project manager. "I told 'em to rip it up, boys. I want four lanes, not two!" I'll even roll down the window and yell at the guys, "I said I wanted twelve-inch corrugated pipe, not six-inch!" My encouragement to all the men out there is "Sell it!" If you want a great marriage, start making stuff up.

Construction zones are callbacks for our marriage. Many times I simply say, "I have too much going on this week to get involved in this project." Amy responds with, "I understand." I spent the first half of our marriage giving answers, when all I needed to do was listen. Amy didn't need me to solve her problems or to finish projects for the Missouri Department of Transportation. She wanted to talk. When I listened with eagerness, our marital satisfaction skyrocketed.

Do you listen with your spouse in mind or are you always the center of the conversation?

What's more important for your relationship: connection, information, or giving answers?

When your spouse speaks, do you think about your next point? Do you reframe the conversation back to you?

Is your communication style one that draws your spouse in or sends him or her away?

Do disagreements over mundane issues sabotage the fun in your marriage?

This next question is for you only, not your spouse. Don't answer it for each other. Let it be a heart check for you.

On a scale of 1 to 10, how good a listener are you?

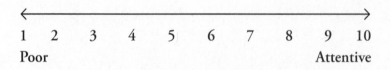

Last year I asked my son and Amy, "On a scale of 1 to 10, how good a listener am I?" They both gave me a 5. That was a blow. I asked what I needed to do better.

Amy said, "When we have your undivided attention, you listen well. I'd give you an 8. But you have too much going on inside that brain of yours."

Carson said, "Dad, the next time I ask for money, I need you to listen." He listened to my request with himself in mind.

Assuming each one of us needs to be heard, what type of listener are you?

There are many types of poor listeners. This by no means is an exhaustive list, but it does help pinpoint where we need work.

The Nodder is the listener who took a management course at work that taught how to be emotionally responsive when someone is talking. As people share, listeners give cues to let the other person know they are hearing and tracking with what's being said. The Nodder takes it too far and gives a nod to each statement made. This is a mark of insincere listening.

The Eye-Roller shows contempt. In my opinion, out of all fifteen bad listeners on this list, this is the most disrespectful listener. The eye-roll shoots right past your stories, ideas, and opinions and goes straight to your character. It attacks the core of your personhood. The eye-roll screams, "You don't matter."

The Bored listener has a difficult time connecting with body language and facial expressions. The vibe is, "I don't want to be here," or "I'd rather be somewhere else, doing something else."

I have a stoic friend who is a kind man. On family vacations, his family asks, "Dad, are you having a good time?"

He's quick to respond, "Yes, why do you ask?"

"You look totally bored," they answer.

His wife reminds him, "Tell your face that you're happy."

The Distracted listener comes in two forms. One, they are distracted by their environment (people, devices, settings, etc.).

Two, they are distracted in their minds (thoughts, lists, errands, etc.). In either case, lack of focus keeps them from dialing into their spouse's words and feelings.

The Eye-Wanderer is on the lookout for something better to do or someone else to engage in conversation. They look over your shoulder to see who's coming. When an eye-wanderer glazes over but then lights up when someone else walks by, it's hard not to take that personally.

The Watch-Glancer needs or wants to be somewhere else. As the little girl on *Full House* would say, "How rude!" A quick glance at the watch says to your spouse, "I need you to wrap this up," or "You've taken enough of my time."

The Scroller has the gall to pull out a device and scroll social media in the middle of the conversation. Amy and I constantly remind ourselves that we are the first generation of parents to raise children with devices, figuring it out as we go along.

However disconcerting this feels, we must remember that the next generation uses technology to contribute to the conversation. We bring in social media posts, YouTube videos, memes, and texts to share with family and friends. I have to laugh thinking about those who choose to not be on social media at all, but have a spouse who sits in the passenger's seat or the La-Z-Boy next to them sharing every post and detail of another's life.

The One-Upper is the competitive listener. They've met more famous people, been to more beautiful destinations, and purchased more extravagant items than you. In marriage, the One-Upper tries to outdo the other spouse. Comparing your strengths to your spouse's weaknesses fills you with pride. Remember that you're teammates, so there's no need to compete against each other.

The One-Downer is close to the One-Upper, but going in the opposite direction. They make their lives appear more difficult than yours. If you come home from work and say, "I had a rough day," the One-Downer spouse responds with, "You think your day was rough? You should see what I had to put up with."

Have you ever posted a picture on Facebook or Instagram of your family vacation? It doesn't have to be a fancy vacation in an exotic location to receive a comment like, "It sure must be nice to go on vacation. I can't remember the last time I went on vacation. Wish we had the money to afford that." That's the One-Downer. If you're sick, the One-Downer has been way sicker. If you got in a car accident and rolled your car three times, they rolled four times.

The Over-Validator already experienced everything you are going through at this very moment. They don't try to outdo or undercut your feelings, but they "know exactly what you're going through."

The Bottom-Liner needs you to cut to the chase. This is a time-oriented listener who needs enough, not too much, information to get the gist. Even if you are a good communicator and cut to it, they will cut you off when they feel you should be done. Beyond the basics, they hear, "Blah, blah, blah."

The Sentence-Completer fills in the blanks for you before you get there. You would think one needs history with someone to do this, but I've met strangers skilled at this. They turn conversations into guessing games.

I say, "Last week, we went to . . ." and the sentence-completer says, "Store?" "Church?" "Work?"

Recently a Sentence-Completer told me she fills in the blanks to add energy to the conversation. That's one way of looking at it.

The Interviewer asks lots of questions. Instead of letting you direct the flow, they come with an agenda. This tends to rush the conversation and drain the energy from the room. Instead of letting it flow, you start to wonder, "Am I giving this person the answers they are looking for?"

Like when someone asks you, "Where do you see yourself in five years?" There's not a right or wrong answer, but the weight of that question paralyzes some. If I don't have an answer, I'll come across as lacking ambition. If I answer slowly, they'll think I'm indecisive. If I answer too quickly with lofty goals, they may question my motives.

The Debater needs to know where you got your information and how long you've thought about this. Their facial expressions lead you to believe they doubt you. I've learned this type of listener may simply enjoy the free-for-all format more than right or wrong answers. These are usually the witty ones, quick on their feet.

The Hijacker never lets you finish a story. Their story is more interesting than yours and they're going to stop you and share it. When I'm with a Hijacker, I keep my statements short and avoid stories altogether. Why make this listener work for the microphone? Just give it to them.

Ready for a Change?

After twenty-three years of marriage, Amy and I are still developing our shared sense of humor. Better listening skills will help me mine our marriage for comedy gold. In the previous chapter we talked about observational humor. Your spouse has plenty to say. There's a good chance something funny could pop into the conversation at any moment. But you've got to be listening to what they say. This is a good time for the "funny" spouse to help the "non-funny" spouse. Find humor in something your spouse says and give it back to him or her with, "See, you're funnier than you think."

It's hard to observe Amy when my mouth is running. For the better part of a year now, listening is the sacred echo in my marriage and life. A sacred echo is God getting your attention through His Word and others in your life. When I told my friend David about my goal of better listening, he said, "That will be a nice change." Ouch. Truth stings and I can always count on this friend to give it to me.

As a nation, our listening skills need work. We get our news today from algorithms and cable news networks that reinforce our biases, which means we only listen to news we agree with. How does that work in my marriage? Do I only listen to Amy when I agree with her? There is no skill in that. The real skill comes in listening to your spouse when you disagree.

Jesus said, "If you love those who love you, what reward do you have? Do not even the tax collectors do the same? And if you greet only your brothers, what more are you doing than others? Do not even the Gentiles do the same?" (Matthew 5:46-47). The real skill lies in loving the EGR (Extra Grace Required) people. The same goes for listening. It's easy for me to talk politics with my dad because we share the same worldview. Ask me to sit and listen to someone attacking my worldview, and that's hard. I've found that humor, appropriately crafted and delivered, can lessen the tension of even the most heated debates.

Amy and I share the same worldview, vote for the same candidates, and agree on most every issue, like gun control, labor unions, the national anthem, and the unborn. We like a peaceful family table, but there are plenty of times when family and friends bring up a hot-button political issue. Amy and I enjoy taking turns playing devil's advocate. We like to argue for the other side. If we side with an extended member of the family on an issue we don't agree with, the shock leads to laughter. You can see it on the faces gathered around the table. "Yeah right, we all know you don't believe that at all, but thanks for playing."

It's easy to have a great conversation with your spouse when you are in lockstep together. But what do you do when you completely disagree on an issue and a decision needs to be made? Do you both walk away feeling like losers, or do you work through it?

Great communication begins with great listening, not formulating great points. Listening to her when you agree with her is for amateurs. Listening to her when you disagree is for professionals.

When a conflicted couple walks into my office, I like to picture them in football jerseys. Is one wearing a Minnesota Vikings jersey and the other a Green Bay Packers jersey? If so, I want to help them both wear the purple Vikings jersey. Sorry, Wisconsin friends, but I have to say that for my father-in-law, Minnesota's biggest fan.

Pretend the conflict is on the fifty-yard line. Opponents come at it from opposite ends of the field. Teammates come at it from the same end zone. Your spouse is your teammate, not your opponent. When you disagree, don't fight over who is right. Start with playing the game on the same team. Teammates often disagree about what routes to run, which team members to play when, and how to cover a guy on defense, but they have the same goal: to win the game together. I've never tried this, but I'm wondering if I should keep two matching sports jerseys in my office, and instead of sitting on the couch discussing issues, invite the couple out for a game of flag football—me and one of our elders on one team, the couple on the other. I, of course, would choose our elder who was a college kicker and was invited to try out for the Green Bay Packers.

This is why I like to help couples talk about money. I am convinced this is the hardest subject for any couple to discuss. It's deeply personal. If they can talk about money with one another in a safe and honoring way, they can talk about almost anything. In other words, if you create a teammate environment in your marriage around money, you can talk about sex, in-laws, parenting styles, faith, and jobs in an honoring way too.

We live in a hostile society. We need to lighten up. When you want to get your voice heard or make a point, boycott! Right? In relationships we have another word for it. It's called withdrawal. I won't engage with you until you come around to my way of thinking. We boycott businesses so they feel it on their bottom line. We withdraw from spouses so it affects them enough to change. Both boycotts and withdrawal don't work.

Remember when people were outraged at comments about marriage voiced by Dan Cathy, CEO of Chick-fil-A? Folks called for a boycott. For weeks after that boycott, I steered clear of Chick-fil-A because the car lines wrapped around the parking lot and into the streets. They received a huge spike in business from that boycott.

Soon after that, citizens called for a boycott of the NFL. Not to get too controversial, but let me ask you this. Are you able to listen to an NFL player who takes a knee? I can. I believe Christians should be known for great conversations, not boycotts. You can't have a conversation without listening.

I tend to withdraw from my wife when conflict hits. When Amy and I disagree, I retreat to another room. I sometimes stir it up a bit, and then I go to the other room. I take it to the level I can handle, then make a dramatic exit. My physical withdrawal removes my lightheartedness immediately. I'd like to say I am contemplating or praying, but to be honest I'm usually sulking. Humor and laughter play a key role in the process of making up. When appropriate humor gently works its way back into the conversation, we both know the reconciliation is working. Laughter serves as a barometer in these situations. It keeps track of the ups and downs of the conversation.

A better approach for me would be to stay and listen, not leave and sulk. My exit and nonverbals communicate . . .

- "I'm done listening to this."
- "You can join me when you agree with me."
- "I'll be in the other room when you are ready to apologize."
- "You need some time to calm down and see this from my point of view."

The NFL boycott felt a lot like a couple's fight to me.

- "I won't participate with you until you start showing some respect."
- "Change, and I'll be back."
- "I don't care what started all of this, I will end it."

In the fall of 2017, when the NFL boycott hit, I was at a marriage retreat in Maryland. It was a diverse retreat with African American congregations, charismatic congregations, and folks from Pennsylvania Dutch, Mennonite, and Amish country.

Right before my last message at the retreat, I taught on the six levels of communication. I spoke to couples on the value of listening in marriage. We laughed and had fun together, until I mentioned the Take the Knee movement.

I said, "You know this issue with the NFL taking the knee? I believe we need to have a good, healthy conversation. Let's try to understand what the players who take a knee are saying." The room fell silent. My three to five laughs a minute during this session were sucked right out of the room. The air was thick. There was no laughter on the jokes to follow. I got a couple of *amens* on my statement, but even those were under fear of judgment.

After the session, a Korean War veteran approached me. He said, "Pastor, I've loved everything about this weekend, but I couldn't disagree with you more on the NFL Take the

Knee." He shared a few other thoughts as I listened. After all, I just finished a session on listening.

When he was done, I said, "Sir, I want to say two things. First of all, thank you for your service to our country. I come from Branson, Missouri, which is the most honoring city in the country when it comes to our veterans. My grandfathers and Amy's grandfathers all served in World War II. We are grateful for your service." Then I said, "I'm one pastor who has been teaching my son and daughter, from a very small age, that when the national anthem plays, you stand up, take off your hat, and you place your hand over your heart until it is done. So I've been teaching that to my kids, sir. I don't think you're going to meet a more patriotic pastor than me. But the second thing I would like to share is that you are validating the very point I was trying to make."

He said, "What's that?"

I said, "You are telling me that you disagree with me, and yet I never shared my opinion on Take the Knee. That was the point I was trying to make. That's where we are with our families, marriages, and nation today. We are telling friends, spouses, family members. and fellow citizens that we don't agree with them, and we don't even know what they believe. There is no harm in listening."

This precious veteran stood there stunned. I didn't mean to "catch" him or trap him, but I wanted us all to learn this valuable lesson.

I asked him, "Do you mind if I share our conversation at the beginning of the next session?" I took his silence as consent.

My next session started with, "How many of you disagree with my stance on Take the Knee?" Hands went up all over the room. I asked, "Would someone be willing to come up and share with the group my opinion?" No one came forward.

For the record, since I've never been one to shy away from my opinion, I still believe when the national anthem is played, you should stand up to respect those who have fought for that flag to show honor and respect, but it doesn't mean we can't have a conversation.

Healthy people are not threatened by the opinions of others. The Scripture teaches us that wise people listen: "A fool takes no pleasure in understanding, but only in express- ing his opinion" (Proverbs 18:2). I don't have to agree with the NFL player in order to understand the NFL player. When I disagree with the NFL player, it doesn't mean I hate him. When I listen, it says, "You matter to me and I want to know what you are thinking and why."

"The purpose in a man's heart is like deep water, but a man of understanding will draw it out" (Proverbs 20:5). That heart is full of beliefs about life, God, church, people, work, money, race, injustice, and equality. Your spouse's heart is like deep waters. Your spouse's parents, pastors, teachers, coaches, family members, peers, and neighbors wrote messages on the tablet of the heart. Messages form when we believe what others repeat over and over again about us. These messages mold and shape our feelings.

For example, if you grew up hearing, "You'll never amount to anything," you probably feel and believe you are worthless.

If you grew up hearing, "Why can't you be more like your brother?" you probably believe and feel that you don't measure up.

If you grew up hearing, "If I've told you once, I've told you a thousand times," you might feel like a failure.

If you grew up hearing, "You got your anger from your father," you now feel judged.

If you grew up hearing, "You were a mistake. We never meant to have you," you now feel defective or unwanted.

We bring the messages that come from our parents into our marriages. Each marriage has two families of origin at play. While the messages from our family of origin are important, over the years there are messages spouses send each other that either shoot down or confirm our insecurities. Cultivating a shared sense of humor and a laughter-filled marriage facilitates open, understanding, person-valuing communication.

An understanding spouse listens for feelings that flow from the messages of the heart. Loving husbands seek to draw these out of their wives. Solomon sought to draw out the Shulammite woman when he said,

> Oh my dove, in the clefts of the rock,
>   in the crannies of the cliff,
> let me see your face,
>   let me hear your voice,
> for your voice is sweet,
>   and your face is lovely.
>
> SONG OF SOLOMON 2:14

"My dove" is a great nickname for your wife. There are many ways to say it, especially if you include flirtatious giggles and sweet nothings. What are some of your playful, silly, or flirtatious pet names for each other? Take a moment and think of some new ones. Guys, if you don't have a pet name for your wife, you may want to start with "my dove." Use it to woo, build up, and draw her out.

A dove responds to gentleness. She is hidden from him, so he pursues her with tenderness and desire. He wants to get to know her. His request to see her face and hear her voice is answered because he sees her face and calls it lovely, and hears her voice and calls it sweet.

You know who else hangs out in the hiding places of the mountainside? Mountain lions, snakes, and rams. Solomon chose none of those as a word picture. He chose the cooing of a dove. When your wife reveals the "deep waters" of her heart, receive her like a dove. When you want to find out what else is in her heart, call out with the dove call.

The dove call sounds something like this: "Coo, coo." Try it. Husband, the next time you want to enter into a deep conversation with your wife, simply call, "Coo, coo."

When Amy tries to have a conversation with me from across the house, all I hear is, "Mfern dwerthy smossy tossy linee gewwwww?" I can tell it's a question, but can't understand a word she says. Next time your wife calls from across the house, don't yell back, "What?" Instead call for her, "Coo, coo." She'll hear, "I want to hear your voice and see your face."

I taught this to Trinity Church in Lake Charles, Louisiana, and one of their hunters approached me after the session and said, "Pastor, you do that coo-cooing around here and you'll get shot." Warning heeded.

One very important warning comes with the "coo, coo." It is very different from "cuckoo," which means "crazy." You do not want to call your wife into conversation with "Cuckoo"! If you did, she might turn on you like a bad hot dog. It is also very different from "Who, who," which is the sound an owl makes.

Your wife may share stuff from her deep waters that shocks you. Go beyond her words to discover feelings. Go beyond her feelings to discover the messages written there years prior.

Ask her questions about her home growing up, school, church, and extended family. There is a lot to learn in the stories she shares. Lean in and draw her out. Listening to your spouse's opinion says, "What you think matters." Listening screams, "You matter to me."

The *Harvard Business Review* refers to this type of listening as "active listening." In an article called "What Great Listeners Actually Do," they released their findings after studying 3,492 participants in a development program where they helped managers become better coaches. They discovered that the most effective listeners (the top 5 percent of the group) draw others out by . . .

- periodically asking questions to promote discovery and insight

- making the conversation a positive experience for the other person
- conveying support and confidence[1]

This is in contrast to what most people consider good listening skills. Most people believe good listeners . . .

- remain silent when others are speaking
- engage with nonverbals
- repeat what others say word for word

Great listening requires more than silence, the occasional head nod, and a few words to show retention. Great listening requires emotional safety and what Dr. Sue Johnson calls "emotional responsiveness."

Dr. Johnson, a clinical psychologist and author of *Hold Me Tight: Seven Conversations for a Lifetime of Love*, is quoted in *Time* magazine's article titled "The Science behind Happy Relationships":

The most important thing we've learned, the thing
that totally stands out in all of the developmental
psychology, social psychology and our lab's work
in the last 35 years is that the secret to loving
relationships and to keeping them strong and vibrant
over the years, to falling in love again and again, is
emotional responsiveness.[2]

This is why quiet chuckles, secret smiles, subtle winks, quirky glances, and sweet little inside jokes add to this emotional bond and in the give-and-take of communication. Again, when Amy and I talk, it's not just about interviewing one another for information. It's about forming a deeper bond and building our shared sense of humor.

Amy and I took our annual abandon this year in Knoxville, Tennessee. One night after dinner, we walked back to the hotel and along the way passed a coffee shop hosting an open-mic stand-up comedy night. My wife lit up and said, "You should totally do this! Please?"

My immediate and final answer was, "No way!"

"Oh, come on, it will be hilarious," she prodded.

"Yeah, for *you*," I said.

We peered through the window and saw a young lady on stage telling jokes. There was no laughter, sounds, or expressions coming from the thirty people in the crowd. We saw lots of distracted, bored, watch-glancing, and scrolling listeners. This coffee shop may be the historical site where the term "tough crowd" originated.

It took me back to some tough speaking environments I have experienced in the past. People eating at fundraisers is a tough gig, especially when the dessert comes. No one pays attention to a speaker when tiramisu shows up. Monday morning church staff meeting after a busy, multi-service Sunday is another tough crowd. They'd rather have the day off.

Not that we should live for it, but preachers, teachers,

speakers, and comedians do look for responsiveness in the crowd. Cues from the crowd let us know where people are at and what we can do to adjust our communication to engage them.

Your spouse wants to know you are tuned in and fully present. Dr. Johnson says, "The $99 million question in love is, 'Are you there for me?'"[3] Our listening skills are a barometer of marital health. They let us know how the relationship is going.

Dr. Gary Smalley called this "emotional safety." He taught me how to be a safe spouse. He shared with me, "Amy will automatically want to open up to you and share, if she knows you receive well. That is safety." The opposite of safety is judgment. If Amy shares and I critique her every word or shut down her feelings, she won't be eager to share with me in the future. Safety makes your spouse feel protected, not vulnerable.

Remember the scene in the movie *Patch Adams* where Patch decides to spend the rest of his life helping people? He announces to his therapist: "I want to help people. . . . I want to listen, really listen to people." His therapist says, "That's what I do." Patch confronts him with the truth that he stinks at it and says, "You don't even look at people when they're talking."[4]

Listening starts with looking. The eyes of the listener connect and say, "I am fully present and ready to hear what's on your heart."

When Amy rated me a five listener, I knew immediately there was more I could do to increase marital satisfaction.

We experienced high levels of marital satisfaction already, but how great could it be if I became a listening professional? She told me once, "There's no one in life I laugh with more than you." We do have fun, but better listening skills make it more fun. Even in our most serious of conversations, we listen to one another with gentle, subtle, shared looks and words of amusement that indicate "I hear you," "I get you," and "I've got your back."

From that personal challenge, I created The Ten Commandments for Professionally Listening to My Wife. This list is personal, but feel free to rip it off and make it your own.

1. What you hear shalt be more important than what I say. My approach gets me in more trouble than my opinion. Sharing my thoughts on an issue requires an approach void of sarcasm, belittling, and contempt.

2. I shalt listen for your feelings when you share your opinions and we make decisions. Yes, we need to make a decision, but I won't do it at the expense of you and your feelings. I have found that when Amy feels listened to prior to a decision, she's open to several different options. When I don't listen, no option feels right.

3. I shalt validate your feelings even when I disagree with your opinions. Understanding how you feel does not mean I agree with your opinion. Listening does not mean I need to solve a problem. Listening does not mean I'm right and you're wrong. When I disagree with you it doesn't mean I hate you. "I don't agree with you" doesn't mean "I don't love you" or "Our marriage isn't working." Marriage works best when you stop trying to change the way your spouse feels, thinks, speaks, and acts.

4. I shalt listen to your opinions without seeing them as an attack on mine. I don't need to bring a sword and shield to every discussion. I am laying down all weapons prior to the conversation.

5. I shalt listen with you, not myself, in mind. How does this issue or decision affect you? What work will this place on you? Months from now, will you be happy with the decision we made?

6. I shalt not go to the other room to avoid conflict. I know withdrawal is my flight response. I choose to engage.

7. I shalt remain silent when you speak. I will live by the words of Proverbs 17:28, "Even a fool who keeps silent is considered wise; when he closes his lips, he is deemed intelligent."

8. I shalt be expressive with my facial expressions. Since "bright eyes gladden the heart" (Proverbs 15:30, NASB), I will meet you with excitement. I will send you emotional cues that let you know I am listening and glad to be there.

9. I shalt be the last to speak. This doesn't mean I need the last word. Not at all. I want to hear you out before I contribute my two cents. "If one gives an answer before he hears, it is his folly and shame" (Proverbs 18:13).

10. I shalt be kind. When I do share my opinions, it will be with kind words. "Gracious words are like a honeycomb, sweetness to the soul and health to the body" (Proverbs 16:24).

Helping Your Spouse Win Every Argument with Improv Skills

Second to our favorite comedy technique, the callback, we love improv. This one skill is the most practical way we know to get on the same page as a couple even when we disagree. Our opposite opinions on issues do not prevent us from helping each other win in conversation.

The number one rule of improvisational comedy is agreement. *You respond to everything said with "Yes, and . . ."* You must agree or you block the conversation. Improv is a team sport, as is marriage. Whatever idea, suggestion, topic, or opinion your spouse throws out, return with "Yes, and _____." You must agree with an affirming statement. Negativity sucks the life out of the conversation, killing intimacy.

We recently tested this with our friends Andy and Stephanie Watson. In the summer of 2018, I taught the couples at Kanakuk Family Kamp in Branson, Missouri, how to communicate using improvisational comedy skills. Andy and Stephanie were in the session and took notes.

An hour after the session, I overheard them discussing tattoos. In jest, Stephanie told Andy she wanted to get a tattoo. All I heard Andy say was, "Absolutely not." I took this as my moment to experiment.

"Why don't you both improv this and see where it goes," I said. Stephanie was game, but Andy was closed.

"Aww, come on, it will be fun," I begged. Stephanie got it right away, but Andy needed some help with affirming statements.

Stephanie: "I want a tattoo."

Andy: "Yes, and you should get a tiger."

Stephanie: "Yes, and I would want it sepia-toned."

Andy: "Yes, and because you are an artist, I can see why you would want one."

Stephanie: "Yes, and I could put it somewhere no one sees."

Andy: "Yes, and I love you just the way you are."

This led to several outbursts of laughter and a whole lot of fun for everyone who witnessed it. This is a fantastic tool for lightening up tense conversations with good-natured silliness and humor. Two people with different opinions on tattoos getting along in a whimsical conversation. This is possible for any couple on any issue.

Funny thing is, Stephanie doesn't even want a tattoo. She likes to instigate fun by poking the bear.

Andy, the next time Stephanie brings up tattoos, don't let it get to you. With an inviting glance, look right in her eyes and say, "Coo, coo."

And remember, it's "Coo, coo," not, "Cuckoo," even when discussing a tattoo.

Your Laughter Score

For a possible 20,000 points,

1. Improv Something Easy

- Pick a food or meal your spouse loves and you can't stand.

- Ask him/her to give you a few reasons why he/she loves it.

- Between descriptions and reasons, use "Yes, and . . ." affirming statements to convince your spouse that you love that food or meal too.

My attempt at humor . . .

Fell flat .... 0 points
Made my spouse smirk .... 1,000 points
Made my spouse smile .... 2,000 points
Made my spouse snicker .... 3,000 points
Made my spouse giggle .... 4,000 points
Made my spouse chuckle .... 5,000 points

Made my spouse cackle ....6,000 points
Made my spouse belly laugh.......................7,000 points
Made my spouse howl...............................8,000 points
Made my spouse shriek ....9,000 points
Made my spouse die laughing...................10,000 points

_____ Her Score _____ His Score

The next time I attempt this humor, I will

_____

2. Improv Something Controversial or Difficult

CONTROVERSIAL

- Pick something from the news or headlines that you both agree on.

- Ask your spouse to play the devil's advocate.

- Each of you make one statement at a time using "Yes, and . . ." statements.

- (Caution: Refrain from belittling the other point of view.)

DIFFICULT

- Agree on the issue and write it here _____
_____.

(Examples: spending habits, parenting styles, in-laws)
The greater the specificity the better.

- Use "Yes, and . . ." statements to affirm one another's point of view.

- Give each other credit for trying. Some words and statements will cross your spouse's lips for the very first time in your marriage.

My attempt at humor . . .

Fell flat...0 points
Made my spouse smirk.............................. 1,000 points
Made my spouse smile...............................2,000 points
Made my spouse snicker............................3,000 points
Made my spouse giggle..............................4,000 points
Made my spouse chuckle............................5,000 points
Made my spouse cackle ....6,000 points
Made my spouse belly laugh......................7,000 points
Made my spouse howl ....8,000 points
Made my spouse shriek ....9,000 points
Made my spouse die laughing.................. 10,000 points

_____ Her Score _____ His Score

The next time I attempt this humor, I will

_____

Write your scores on page 206, too.

Conversation Starters and a Few More Laughs

- Circle the listening style(s) that best describe how you listen.

  A. The Nodder
  B. The Eye-Roller
  C. The Bored
  D. The Distracted
  E. The Eye-Wanderer
  F. The Watch-Glancer
  G. The Scroller
  H. The One-Upper
  I. The One-Downer
  J. The Over-Validator
  K. The Bottom-Liner
  L. The Sentence-Completer
  M. The Interviewer
  N. The Debater
  O. The Hijacker

- What car best describes your approach to conflict? Why?

  A. Ford Explorer
  B. Dodge Ram
  C. Ford Focus
  D. The Rambler
  E. Chevy Spark

- Why are we threatened by the differing opinions of others?

- Do you feel that your spouse understands your feelings when he or she doesn't agree with your opinions?

- Is it possible to make a major decision when you don't agree?

CHAPTER 5

Holy Shiplap, Chip!

For a marriage to sing and dance, for two
people to make beautiful music together, they need to play,
not work, at their marriage.

LEONARD SWEET

Life does not cease to be funny when people die
any more than it ceases to be serious when people laugh.

GEORGE BERNARD SHAW

CHIP GAINES IS ruining my marriage. My wife loves Joanna Gaines, but I can't keep up with Chip. This down-to-earth couple is a powerful force for the Kingdom and they have a great testimony with their show *Fixer Upper* on HGTV. Their marriage is strong, and it comes through the screen with every home they restore.

Nonetheless, Chip, you're killing me!

Not only is he good with tools, excited about projects, and open to major changes given to him on a whim by Joanna, he loves everything about a honey-do list. He tells jokes, dances, and gets plain silly in almost every interview I've ever seen.

My wife can't get enough of this show. The Gaineses fuel her passion and vision for our home.

I came home from work one night and found Amy staring at a wall in our dining room. I asked, "How was your day?" She stood silent as she studied the wall between the dining room and kitchen. In the quiet, I gazed upon the wall as well.

"What are we looking at, my love?" I asked before having my first question answered.

She said, "After dinner, I think we should move that wall."

I couldn't breathe. There were no words. I'd already planned on checking the garden after dinner, but starting a major renovation of our home was not in the plan.

Holy Shiplap, Chip! Do you have any idea how you empower wives with grandiose plans? A quick Google search rescued me that night, and to this day. I found a term that saved my marriage: "load bearing." Every wall in our home is load bearing. You mess with one and the entire house comes down.

Chip Gaines is a great husband, father, and follower of Christ, but he could let some of us off the hook in his interviews and books with a nod and a simple, "I know my passion for fixing up houses is not every husband's cup of tea." That's all I need, Chip.

Amy and I learned early in marriage that honoring and enjoying the differences between us is the fast track to marital satisfaction. We can waste time trying to change each other, or we can have fun with the quirkiness in each of us. We can live in frustration or fascination. The choice is ours. Embracing our differences validates how God wired us. When I appreciate the differences between the two of us, I see Amy as personally autographed by God.

We Enjoy Our Differences around the Home

Our home is an extension of my wife. I'll never change that. Instead, I do everything in my power to make it a castle fit for the queen. Two things make that a challenge. I'm not handy, and I dread construction projects. I lack both skills and passion.

When our daughter, Corynn, turned one, we threw her a birthday bash like any first-time parents would. As President Donald J. Trump says, "It was HUUUUUUGE!" We lived in a small home, so we cleaned out the garage, set up tables, and made room for our little princess's royal guest list. The ball took months of planning. The theme was bees, and our home was all abuzz looking forward to August 4, 2004.

On August 1, I asked Amy, "What else can I do to help you get ready for Corynn's party?"

Her shoulders slumped in relief and she said, "Thank you so much, babe. Would you mind laying ceramic tile in the kitchen and breakfast nook for me?"

She wasn't attempting humor. Her enthusiasm and confidence in my skills and abilities leaves me speechless.

"Let me rephrase the question," I said. "Do you want me to pick up the balloons?"

I don't think it is possible to be on two more opposite

pages than we are when it comes to our home. I have laid tile before, so I shared with her the timeline:

"Ceramic tile is a multistep process, sweetie . . .

Step 1: I need to rip up the linoleum.

Step 2: Lay backer board with thin set and wait twenty-four hours for it to dry.

Step 3: Lay tile and wait another twenty-four hours to dry.

Step 4: Grout tile and wait another twenty-four hours to dry."

"So you're saying you would need at least three days?" she asked after calculating. Unbelievable. I'm thinking it is way too much work and time to have ready for the party; she is seeing if we can squeeze it in. She is the optimist. And this is another example of her thinking I am an expert on everything.

Amy and I bought our first home in 1998, during our seminary years in Dallas. It was a $90,000 cookie-cutter home in a subdivision of 200 homes. We chose some upgrades, but most of the features of the home were basic starter fixtures.

One night shortly after moving in, Amy and I enjoyed an evening at home, watching one of our favorite television programs. Halfway through the program, Amy jumped up and announced, "I can't sit in this living room one more minute!"

"What's wrong?" I asked.

"Doesn't it bother you that the doorknobs in this room are shiny brass and the ceiling fan is brushed nickel? What were the builders thinking?" she exclaimed.

My eyes focused on the fan, then the door, then the fan

and then the door in rapid fire. I could not process what had her so alarmed. We had just watched an intense suspense movie, and I had no idea that for the first thirty minutes of the show, Amy could not focus on the plot or the characters because of the mismatched doorknobs and ceiling fan.

Any idea what our first errand was that Saturday? You guessed it. We were at the home improvement store purchasing brushed-nickel doorknobs. Amy was at peace. Well, at least until that night. A new doorknob was on a door between our bedroom and the living room. And the ceiling fan in our master bedroom was shiny brass. On Sunday we were back at the home improvement store buying a brushed-nickel ceiling fan for our room. For many, not all, women, the home is an extension of who they are, and the little details can make a big difference when it comes to their comfort level.

Have you ever headed out the door and heard your wife say, "Oh, I forgot to wash the dishes," or "I didn't make the bed"? It's really hard for a woman to walk out when things are undone. It's almost as if a part of *her* is undone.

I leave the house without worrying about the dishes, but Amy can't. When I understand this difference, I am better equipped to love and serve her in a way that makes her feel comfortable and more secure in our relationship and home. I prefer to serve her, and refuse to change her.

Amy has more love languages than just acts of service and quality time. One of her favorite love languages is saying, "Pitch, pitch, pitch." She loves to throw away clutter. Deep in her heart rests the belief, "If you haven't used it in the past six months, throw it away." This is how she loves me and how I show her love.

She shows me love every time she gets rid of stuff. Her eyes light up and her heart leaps when she sees me carrying out to the car a bag of clothes I no longer wear. I show her love by cleaning out my closet.

Spring cleaning is a weeklong lovefest at our home. She walks around the garage holding up one item at a time asking, "When was the last time you used this?"

"That's a hammer," I say with puppy dog eyes.

"Are you still using it?" She rephrases her question.

"Every home is entitled to one hammer. It behooves us to keep one on hand in case something comes up, like removing a wall after dinner," I say as she tosses it into the fifty-five gallon garbage can. Again, I don't try to change her, but I wait for her to go to bed, then I sneak out in the wee hours of the morning and save my stuff.

I walked into our master closet the other day to see Amy staring at one of her sweaters. I thought she was looking for snags, but she was deep in thought.

"Whatcha doin', babe?" I asked.

"I'm wondering if this sweater still sparks joy," she said.

I didn't know what to say, so I probed for greater understanding, "What do you mean?"

"Marie Kondo has a series on Netflix called *Tidying Up with Marie Kondo*. I watched the first two episodes and they were so inspiring. To declutter, she encourages you to hold in your hands one item at a time and ask the question, 'Does this spark joy?' If it does, keep it. If it does not, say, 'Thank you,' give it a kiss, and place it in either the donate or discard pile," she clarified.

I said, "Not sure I can get into that because men ask entirely different questions when we gaze upon an article of clothing. Does it still fit? Does it smell? If the first answer is yes and the second answer is no, we're good to go."

Do you and your spouse enjoy your differences around the house? Do you have speechless moments after requests come flying at you out of left field? Are you grateful for the differences?

In the spirit of Tim McGraw's song "Live Like You Were Dying," I once asked Amy, "What would you do if you had only a year to live?"

Some might say, "Hit the road with family and travel."

Many would choose to live out their days in a quiet place with those closest to them.

Amy said, "I would remodel our house."

I love you, Amy Cunningham!

Every attempt to change your spouse is a complete and total waste of energy and time. You can't change your spouse. You are not responsible for the personality, passions, and giftedness of your spouse. God created your mate in His image. The only choice you have is to either fight it and live in frustration or let it go and have fun with it.

Letting go ain't easy, especially when you are burdened for

the one you love. You desire to help them, but your attempts go unheeded. You know the quality of your spouse's life could be a whole lot better if he or she listened to you.

I've tried for years to teach my entire family how to load a dishwasher. There's a right way and a wrong way to load it. One way gets the dishes clean, all other ways require some utensils and dishes to go through a second time. Who's with me?

When the wooden spoon falls through the top rack, it prevents the spinners from doing what they're supposed to do. You can't cram a cookie sheet on the bottom rack either. If the things that are supposed to spin aren't spinning, the dishes won't get clean.

Your spouse may say, "Please look at the dishwasher— I don't think it's working!"

Inside your head you scream, "It's working just fine! It's user error!"

At dinner my daughter takes a sip of water and says, "Ew, this glass is dirty."

At that very moment I have a choice. I could yell, "It's because you carelessly placed a fork on the top rack." Or I could simply get up and get her a clean glass with water.

I'm not saying my way is the right way, but those are the manufacturer's recommended loading instructions as well.

When the washing machine is shaking violently and everyone in the family assumes it's broken, it ain't broke! It's trying to do two loads of laundry simultaneously. Someone crammed a full load of shirts in on top of a comforter.

When these things happen, take a deep breath. Don't get mad. Go with it. Have fun with it. Enjoying life and marriage is a choice. That means you smile as you take a few items of clothing out or rearrange the spatula and ladle on the top shelf, just as your spouse smiles as he or she overloads the washer and sticks the wooden spoon in vertically. It's all in the decision.

We Enjoy Our Gender Differences Too

We are raising a boy and a girl, and there's a big difference between the two of them. I know it's not popular in our culture, but I'm teaching my children to celebrate the created distinction between male and female. I want my son to embrace his biological sex and marry the opposite sex. The foundation on which we build marriage theology is Genesis 1:27, which says, "So God created mankind in his own image, in the image of God he created him; male and female he created them."

My daughter's elementary school started a watchdog program where each day a dad attended classes and monitored the halls. When it was my turn, I was eager to take the pledge and attend my daughter's kindergarten class.

It was winter and the teacher invited the class to the center rug to listen to a story. She read from a book about winter activities. The girls listened intently on the first couple of rows. The boys sat in the back and role-played each of the activities. They didn't want to hear about snowball fights;

they wanted to go outside and hurl them at someone's face. That was not an option, so they pretended in the back of the room. The teacher said more than once, "Boys, settle down." I shook my head. Do boys need to learn how to be still? Sure. But first, let them be boys.

My friend Chad Phillips and I took our boys to Silver Dollar City when they were ten and eleven years old. We were with them the entire time and their behavior was normal boy behavior for a theme park. Twice within an hour, random senior adults told them, "Settle down." Chad and I shrugged it off. On the third time I told Chad, "If one more person tells our boys to calm down, my angry little preacher voice is going to come out."

Theme parks don't provide a stellar environment for young boys to settle down. Funnel cakes, roller coasters, and spinny rides scream, "Get wound up!"

In their bestselling book, *Brain Sex: The Real Difference Between Men and Women*, Anne Moir and David Jessel write,

A hundred years ago, the observation that men were different from women, in a whole range of aptitudes, skills, and abilities, would have been a leaden truism, a statement of the yawningly obvious.

Such a remark, uttered today, would evoke very different reactions. Said by a man, it would suggest a certain social ineptitude, a *naïveté* in matters of sexual politics, a sad deficiency in conventional wisdom, or a clumsy attempt to be provocative. A woman venturing such an opinion would be scorned as a traitor to her sex, betraying the hard-fought "victories" of recent decades as women have sought equality of status, opportunity and respect.

Yet the truth is that virtually every professional scientist and researcher into the subject has concluded that the brains of men and women are different. There has seldom been a greater divide between what intelligent, enlightened opinion presumes—that men and women have the same brain—and what science knows—that they do not.[1]

This is what I love about my friend Mark Gungor. He assures the men at his Laugh Your Way to a Better Marriage seminar that he will make no attempts to "turn men into women." Mark boldly proclaims and celebrates these differences.

Celebrating the differences between men and women grows curiosity and fascination between a husband and wife. These differences are meant to build up a marriage. If misunderstood or used as an excuse, they lead to frustration and manipulation.

Men tend to be objective and focus on facts. Women tend to be personal and better at expressing their emotions. When the husband and wife get home from work, he's used up most of his words already, but she has some left. She wants to talk and he asks, "What do you want to talk about?"

She responds, "Nothing specific—let's just talk."

In a lot of ways, men are like the inside of a ship. We are compartmentalized. We go to one room and shut the door. Then we go into another room and shut the door and so on. Women are more like a river. They flow. The past, the present, and the future all flow together.

Sometimes a man will come home from work and the wife will ask, "Did you think about me today?" The man will respond, "Well, let me think. I'm sure I did." Like I said, men tend to compartmentalize. When they're at work, they're at work; when they're at home, they're at home.

She Enjoys Massages, I Do Not

My first and last massage was in February 2009 in northern California. What was I thinking allowing California to be the first state to give me a massage? Don't hate me, California, but it was one of the most horrible predicaments of my life.

Amy and I were at a marriage retreat for Cornerstone Church in Livermore. Caren Wolfe, the marriage director at the church, blessed us with a fantastic gift basket. Part of the gift was a couple's massage at the resort.

Rolling my eyes, I looked at Amy and said, "Oh great!" I was grateful for the gesture but had no need to be rubbed on for an hour while lying naked on a table. I immediately went down to the spa to trade it in for an all-day treatment for Amy. The lady at the front desk was quite the saleswoman.

She said, "Do it for your wife, sir." Sure, play the guilt card. I scheduled a 4:00 p.m. massage for the next day.

After one of the most distracting morning sessions of my life, we made our way to the spa at 3:30 that afternoon. When we got there, I was led away to the men's locker room. The young lady pointed to the lockers and requested that I get completely naked and wear the provided robe. My first thought was, *That ain't gonna happen.*

Conference attendees packed the spa that day. That didn't help. Fellowshipping with believers and being called "Pastor" while walking around in a robe is not something we do in the Ozarks.

We started by sipping tea in an Asian-themed cabana with our brothers and sisters in Christ. Yuck! Next, we were summoned from the hallway, alerting some ten couples from the event to the fact that the keynote speaker was only minutes away from lying naked on a table.

Once we got in the room, I took off my robe and jacket. Amy and I lay down on separate tables three feet apart. Amy laughed the entire time. She knew every bone in my body was crying out, "Don't do this!"

Before we went in, I asked her, "Will they touch my butt? That's all I need to know. If they are going to touch my rear end, I'm not doing the massage."

Amy said, "Just tell him not to."

Right. How in the world do I start *that* conversation?

Pretty soon the masseuse and masseur entered the room and turned on some soft music.

My masseur, Steve, started in at my feet and figured out in the first minute that I'm ticklish. As he worked on my legs, he started digging into my thighs with his elbow. I felt a rush of pain and let out several "Oooohs," my cues for him to lighten up. Amy snickered, having a blast with her massage and getting plenty of entertainment from mine. I scored about 136,000 laughter points on that massage.

He asked me two questions during the entire massage. The first question was whether I was ticklish. I thought, *We are not going to start chitchatting right now*. His second question came while he worked on my glutes (which Amy promised would not happen). "Are you athletic?" he asked.

What? Totally inappropriate question! Terrible timing! I was done and ready to bolt.

I survived the torturous fifty minutes. When Steve finished, he laid my robe across my chest and whispered in my ear, "Good night."

I wanted to scream out, "Go away, you sicko!" After he left, I got up and put my robe on. I was sitting in the fetal position at the end of the table when Amy attempted to put her arm around me. I pushed her away and muttered, "Give me a second." Never had I felt so violated.

I have re-gifted every massage I've been given since. Now you know why.

Your Laughter Score

For a possible 20,000 points,

1. Aha Honor Moment. Get face-to-face with your spouse, open your mouth wide, and say, "Whoa! I can't believe I get to be married to you. How did I get so lucky?" Keep laying on the words of high value until you get the desired response.

My attempt at humor . . .

Fell flat .... 0 points
Made my spouse smirk .... 1,000 points
Made my spouse smile .... 2,000 points
Made my spouse snicker .... 3,000 points
Made my spouse giggle .... 4,000 points
Made my spouse chuckle .... 5,000 points
Made my spouse cackle .... 6,000 points
Made my spouse belly laugh .... 7,000 points
Made my spouse howl .... 8,000 points
Made my spouse shriek .... 9,000 points
Made my spouse die laughing .... 10,000 points

_____ Her Score   _____ His Score

The next time I attempt this humor, I will

_____

2. Declutter. Together, walk to a room in your house that you know needs a good cleaning. Start in the master closet, garage, kitchen, basement, or even in front of a drawer in the laundry room. Each of you choose five items to pitch or donate. Your spouse must agree on your choice. The laughs will come when you choose an item for the pure shock of it. Make your case. And feel free to choose a number of items other than five.

My attempt at humor . . .

Fell flat ....0 points
Made my spouse smirk ....1,000 points
Made my spouse smile ....2,000 points
Made my spouse snicker ....3,000 points
Made my spouse giggle ....4,000 points
Made my spouse chuckle ....5,000 points
Made my spouse cackle ....6,000 points
Made my spouse belly laugh ....7,000 points
Made my spouse howl ....8,000 points
Made my spouse shriek ....9,000 points
Made my spouse die laughing ....10,000 points

_____ Her Score   _____ His Score

The next time I attempt this humor, I will

_____

Write your scores on page 206, too.

Conversation Starters and a Few More Laughs

- When is the last time you laughed with one another over a household chore?

- What differences shocked you the most about your spouse at the beginning of your marriage, but now make you laugh together?

- Is this a good time to reconsider the distribution of household chores? Which chores do you enjoy the most? Which ones do you loathe?

- Can you think of a time when love led you to do something awkward or uncomfortable with your spouse?

CHAPTER 6

Every Marriage Is a Duet in Need of Great Backup Singers

We will exult and rejoice in you;
we will extol your love more than wine.

SONG OF SOLOMON 1:4

The person who can bring the spirit of laughter
into a room is indeed blessed.

BENNETT CERF

OUR DEAR FRIENDS Jill and David love to laugh. Our friendship started around a table with great food and laughter years ago, but is now forged through changing seasons, joy, sorrow, and our desire to serve the Lord. I learned recently that a pastor challenged Jill and David to write down names of couples they wanted to invest in. Amy and I were on their list. Jill and David are like backup singers in the duet of our marriage.

They sharpen our marriage. We listen to them. We trust them. We believe God blesses their marriage so they can bless other marriages. What started with laughter grew into a beautiful, life-giving friendship.

Up until this point in the book, we've focused on choosing joy and adding humor and laughter to your marriage. To sustain that, you need friends who believe it is important too. You need backup singers who know how to pursue joy.

The fact is, every marriage has backup singers, intentional or not. Some invited, others uninvited. Some need to be turned down or muted. Others need to be turned way up.

The idea of backup singers comes from the Song of Solomon. This Old Testament book is the duet between King Solomon and the Shulammite woman. Throughout it they sing their love lyrics back and forth to each other. Their song is a beautiful melody of love, romance, passion, intimacy, and commitment.

The Daughters of Jerusalem back up their duet. The first time we hear them harmonizing from the background is in the Song of Solomon 1:4 when they sing, "We will exult and rejoice in you; we will extol your love more than wine . . ." From the moment the Shulammite woman expresses attraction and desire for Solomon in chapter 1 to their conflict after the honeymoon in chapter 5, the Daughters of Jerusalem rejoice in and praise the love of this couple. Every time the Daughters of Jerusalem sing, they are 100 percent for the success of the marriage. How refreshing is that? They seek to build it up, not tear it down.

Do you have singles and other couples in your life that you enjoy spending time with? Who do you laugh with? Who do you roar with? Who refreshes your marriage? With which friends do you end your time together saying, "We need to do that again"?

I have a friend who spent years as the intake director at a residential facility for troubled teens. He once told me that one of the most frustrating aspects of his job was watching God work in the hearts of these teens knowing many of them would return to troubled homes, schools, and neighborhoods. Our environment and those we spend time with shape our lives. Those you spend time with shape your marriage, too.

Do you know who your backup singers are right now? Here is a twofold exercise. Start by taking inventory of family, friends, church members, or coworkers who currently speak into your marriage. They can be couples or singles who are good or bad for your marriage. Second, write down couples you would like to invite to be backup singers. After you write down those speaking into your marriage and those you'd like to invite, assess whether you need to turn them up or down.

If you have a hard time agreeing on which backup singers to turn up and which ones to turn down, don't fret. Leave the check boxes empty for now. As we explore attributes of good backup singers, the answers may become clearer.

Names of Backup Singers	Turn up	Turn down
1.	☐	☐
2.	☐	☐
3.	☐	☐
4.	☐	☐
5.	☐	☐
6.	☐	☐
7.	☐	☐
8.	☐	☐
9.	☐	☐

Do you and your spouse agree with who is on this list?

Do you agree on the ones to turn up and the ones to turn down?

Who you allow to speak into your life is critical for the health and longevity of your marriage. There are four attributes you need to look for in a good backup singer. With your list of backup singers in mind, consider the following attributes of those who bring harmony to your duet.

1. Good Backup Singers Share More in Common with You than Just Laughter

C. S. Lewis once said, "The typical expression of opening Friendship would be something like, 'What? You too? I thought I was the only one.' . . . It is then that true Friendship is born."[1] Laughter bonds us with others and identifies experiences, both good and bad, that we share in common. I remind couples at comedy events that everyone falls in love with the front end of the puppy, and every puppy has a back end. Every couple has back-end stories of times when their marriage hit a rough patch. When a marriage struggles, we tend to fall for the lie that says, "No one understands what I'm going through." Not true. There are couples all around you who have experienced the exact same struggle.

Here's the difference. Some experience struggle, learn from it, and mature. Others throw a pity party, blame others, and learn nothing. Look for mature backup singers.

Laughing with friends is fun, but that says nothing of their ability to get serious and encourage you and your marriage. Laughter helps us identify others we have good chemistry with, but it is not an indicator of wisdom and maturity. Good backup singers know the Lord and are grounded in His Word.

Pay careful attention to who you hang out with and who you listen to. If your friends, coworkers, or siblings are divorced, discern whether their divorce made them wiser or jaded. One study shows that people who had a divorced friend were 147 percent more likely to be divorced than people whose friends' marriages were intact. The study also revealed that a divorced coworker can increase the likelihood of another employee divorcing by 55 percent compared to an employee who works with non-divorced employees. People with a divorced sibling are 22 percent more likely to get divorced than people who don't have divorced siblings.[2] The divorce is not the sole issue; it's the maturity or immaturity that follows.

Immature backup singers need to be turned down and in some cases muted. I almost muted a backup singer on a plane a few years ago, but stopped myself. When I say "muted" I mean literally. I have regrets for not saying or doing something, but then again, I can't meddle in everyone's business.

The lady in the seat behind me was on the phone with a friend and doing all of the talking. My whole body cringed as I listened to her give some of the worst marriage advice I had ever heard in such a condensed period of time. I've heard a lot of terrible marriage advice in my life, but this was like listening to the audiobook for *How to Have a Terrible Marriage for Dummies*.

Here are a few snippets of advice I remember as this woman encouraged her friend to end the marriage:

"You didn't know him all that well before you got married."

"You haven't been married all that long—are you sure you want this to be the rest of your life?"

"Whatever you decide will be the right thing."

"He'll be fine, probably relieved."

"He doesn't like your friends."

I wasn't a big fan of this particular friend either. I was tempted to grab the phone out of her hand and say, "Don't listen to a word your friend said and go find yourself someone who speaks with wisdom and will bless your marriage." Friends make great backup singers when their words and actions are rooted in Scripture, not emotion or experience.

2. Good Backup Singers Esteem Marriage as Highly Valuable

Limit time with those who dishonor marriage. Every follower of Christ is called to esteem marriage as highly valuable. Hebrews 13:4 says, "Let marriage be held in honor among all, and let the marriage bed be undefiled." That means every Christian, whether young or old, single or married, is called to esteem marriage as highly valuable.

Like Solomon and the Shulammite woman, your marriage is surrounded by backup singers. Some of these voices encourage and bless your marriage, while others may lead you to doubt and lose hope.

Bad backup singers bring discord to your duet by saying things like:

- "You never should have married him."
- "She's never going to change."
- "You've tried everything and I think it would be best to end the marriage."
- "You deserve to be happy."
- "You'll find someone else and be better off for it."

Good backup singers say things like:

- "We believe Jesus breathes life into dead people, and we believe He breathes life into dead marriages."
- "Don't lose hope, let's keep praying for your marriage miracle."
- "Have you looked into marriage counseling or a marriage intensive?"
- "Why don't the two of you come over for dinner and let's see what we can do to help you through this."
- "Call me anytime. I'm here for the two of you. I want to help."

After hearing some of these examples of backup singers, revisit the list you started a couple of pages back. Any clarity? Are you settled on which box to check? Is it time to turn down or mute the backup singers that are taking your duet off-key? Turn up the volume on those that know how to honor and bless your marriage.

3. Good Backup Singers Advocate for Both Spouses, Not Just One

Every time you hear the Daughters of Jerusalem in the Song of Solomon, they advocate for marriage, not just one spouse. In chapter 5, Solomon and the Shulammite woman are newlyweds. Like many couples returning from a honeymoon, they find that conflict soon finds its way into their marriage.

The Shulammite woman feels remorse after the fight and

goes in search of Solomon. Along the way, she runs into the Daughters of Jerusalem. Again, we find that they are relentless in promoting oneness in marriage: "Where has your beloved gone, O most beautiful among women? Where has your beloved turned, that we may seek him with you?" (Song of Solomon 6:1).

Notice they didn't say, "He's a creep." "Shame on him for treating you that way." Or "You deserve way better treatment than that." Good backup singers never initiate or engage in a spouse-bashing session. Instead, they say, "What can we do to help?" The Daughters of Jerusalem engage in reconciliation.

This would be a good time to consider your role as a backup singer. Maybe you have a child, sibling, friend, or coworker considering an affair or divorce. What do you say when you get the news someone close to you is in a bad marriage and wants to call it quits?

First of all, you are the first line of defense. Don't resist this opportunity. Listen and validate their feelings, without condoning any bad decisions they make. Don't bash, put down, curse, or justify the words or actions of the other spouse. Remind them of truth. Often a hurting spouse will rewrite history by saying things like, "If she cheated on me that must mean she has never loved me." In that moment, simply say, "That is not true. I've known you two for a long time. You two love each other." Make it your goal to keep lines of communication open so they will continue to lean on you for help.

Second, point them in the right direction. Offer your

support to find good counselors or a marriage intensive pro-gram. Some backup singers have the financial means to pro-vide funds to make this type of help possible. Invite them to attend a small group or Bible study with you. Recommend marriage books, retreats, and conferences. Send the links to websites that offer help to hurting couples. Like the Daughters of Jerusalem, go on a relentless reconciliation mission.

Third, ask them if they believe Jesus Christ was raised from the dead. If they answer "Yes," remind them that the same power that raised Jesus from the dead is the exact same power that raises dead marriages. If they say "No," introduce them to the only One who can save their lifeless soul. If God has the power to breathe life into His dead Son, He has the power to breathe life into your dead marriage.

4. Good Backup Singers Set a Good Example

One senior couple recently said, "In our day, when something was broke, you didn't throw it away, you fixed it." When life throws challenges at you, thank God you have a spouse to face those challenges with you.

Do you know why a couple stays married for fifty-plus years? There are many answers our culture throws at us:

"They are soul mates."

"They are compatible."

"Love."

The correct answer is character. Commitment in marriage

flows from character. You make the decision to honor your vows and love one another in "sickness and health, for richer or for poorer, in good times and in bad, until death do us part." Commitment means choosing to give up other choices. Commitment does not look for greener grass. Where the grass is greener, there is a septic leak. Commitment stays home and waters its own lawn.

Character trumps compatibility in thriving marriages. When you turn on the television and see commercials for online dating sites, you would think compatibility and chemistry are the keys to success in marriage. Not true. Compatibility is not something you find, discover, or test for. You create it over a long period of time. For that reason you need character and the commitment that flows from it.

The knowledge and skills required for marital satisfaction are best lived out in biblical community. That's why a few years ago I challenged the couples of Woodland Hills Family Church to get serious about backup singers. We encouraged our young couples to invite senior couples out on a double date. We hoped that these double dates would lead to on-going relationships in which couples would become backup singers for one another—the kind of backup singers that could be turned up all the way. We equipped the foursomes with some easy conversation starters to get the night rolling. I also challenged the young couples to pick up the check afterward.

Finding great backup singers may take time. Start with

your spouse's friends and see if you jell with the friend's spouse. Church is also a great place to start in a small group or life group. Don't think only of older couples. Look instead for solid, successful marriages no matter what the age of the couple or length of the marriage. Leverage special dinners and holidays to invite potential backup singers onto the stage of your duet. Here are a few of the conversation starters to get the most out of the date:

1. How did you two meet?

2. How long did you date before you married?

3. Tell us about your wedding.

4. Who was in your wedding party?

5. Where did you go on your honeymoon?

6. What one issue drove a wedge between you two in the early years of your marriage?

7. Was there ever a time where you wanted to throw in the towel and give up on marriage?

8. Have family or friends ever discouraged you in your marriage? If so, what did they say? What would you say to them now?

9. Do you have a friend or family member who regularly encourages you in your marriage?

10. How did your parents impact your marriage?

11. Which TV sitcom best represents your marriage and family?

12. Do you have a regular date night? What was your most creative date?

13. What is the best vacation you've been on as a family?

14. What are your favorite travel destinations?

15. What steps are you taking to care for your health?

16. How do you make each other laugh?

17. How do you divide household chores?

Finally, don't get stuck with thinking you only need to befriend other couples. Great backup singers can be any age in any season of life. Don't overlook singles, widows, or widowers. They have much to offer.

My friend Ted Lowe is the founder of Married People, based in Cummings, Georgia. He gets the importance of fun in marriage, and we often work together on projects to help couples enjoy life together. He wrote a blog post called "Why Your Spouse Isn't Enough, and Why They Shouldn't Be" where he gives several good reasons why you and your spouse must broaden your circle. Lowe says, "I don't believe [God] ever intended for us to live in a community of two."[3] I second that.

Your Laughter Score

For a possible 10,000 points,

1. Sing It Like a Country Song. This is a skill I'm proud of, and I use it to ruin my children's cool music. It drives my daughter bonkers when I sing Ed Sheeran songs in a twangy country voice. My thirteen-year-old son loves Frank Sinatra. Carson is an old soul. Whenever I sing "Fly Me to the Moon" or "New York, New York" like Tim McGraw, Carson cringes and says I'm crossing major lines. Ask your spouse to name a current song or a favorite song, then sing a line or two like Garth Brooks. If you try this with Journey, Def Leppard, or Michael Bublé, the laughter will flow through tears.

My attempt at humor . . .

Fell flat...0 points
Made my spouse smirk..............................1,000 points
Made my spouse smile...............................2,000 points
Made my spouse snicker............................3,000 points
Made my spouse giggle..............................4,000 points
Made my spouse chuckle............................5,000 points
Made my spouse cackle ....6,000 points
Made my spouse belly laugh.......................7,000 points
Made my spouse howl ....8,000 points
Made my spouse shriek ....9,000 points
Made my spouse die laughing...................10,000 points

_____ Her Score _____ His Score

The next time I attempt this humor, I will

_____

Write your scores on page 206, too.

Conversation Starters and a Few More Laughs

- What song title best describes your first date? (Earn some extra credit points on this one and sing it.)

  A. "Cold as Ice"
  B. "Jesus, Take the Wheel"
  C. "A Little Less Conversation"
  D. "I Want to Hold Your Hand"

- Which couples are you investing in?

- Think of someone from your past who took your duet off-key. What did they do or say that worked against your marriage?

- Who are you muting?

- Who are you turning up?

CHAPTER 7

Four Habits of
Highly Happy Couples

Finally, brothers, whatever is true, whatever is honorable,
whatever is just, whatever is pure, whatever is lovely, whatever is
commendable, if there is any excellence, if there is anything
worthy of praise, think about these things.

PHILIPPIANS 4:8

Most people would rather be certain
they're miserable than risk being happy.

ROBERT NEWTON ANTHONY

TO KEEP THE HUMOR and laughter flowing in your marriage, you need to identify potential threats to enjoying life together. Laughter was easy early in our marriage. But what comes naturally early on requires us to become intentional later on. It is important to identify some of the potential threats, or roadblocks, to the fun, joy, and laughter you desire. When the fun slows down and laughter is decreasing, you need to pause and ask the question "Why?" Happy couples are vigilant with spotting and removing these road-blocks to fun in marriage.

Dr. Gary Smalley's passion at the Smalley Relationship Center was to increase marital satisfaction and decrease the divorce rate. This mission led him and his son Dr. Greg Smalley to launch a marriage intensive program in Branson, Missouri. It quickly became the premier emergency room for marriages in our country. This program is now Focus on the Family's Hope Restored. These marriage intensive retreats are held at three locations (Branson, Missouri; Greenville, Michigan; and Rome, Georgia). Couples considering separation or filing the papers of divorce find healing and high levels of marital satisfaction through this program. Over 80 percent of the couples that leave the intensive not only stay together, but report levels of marital satisfaction they never dreamed possible.

My twenty-two years of pastoral counseling and marriage ministry finds its roots in what Dr. Gary Smalley and the marriage intensive program taught me. Over the years I've worked with countless couples who desire high levels of marital satisfaction but don't know how to get there. They also have many misconceptions about what it takes to make it happen.

Couples who enjoy life together have a few things in common. They share core beliefs and practices that form lifetime habits. In my work with couples, I've discovered the following four habits help build marital satisfaction, prevent couples from drifting apart, and keep the channel of laughter open.

1. Highly Happy Couples Play as Teammates, Not Opponents

Most of us would agree that God gave us marriage for companionship when He said in Genesis 2:18, "It is not good that the man should be alone; I will make him a helper fit for him." Yet the tone of many marriage books, seminars, ministries, and sermons seems to be "The purpose of marriage is not to make you happy" or "God did not intend for marriage to make you happy." This tone focuses on the "iron sharpens iron" (Proverbs 27:17) aspect of companionship. What about all of the other aspects? Ecclesiastes 4:9-12 clearly lays out many other sides to companionship:

> Two are better than one, because they have a good reward for their toil. For if they fall, one will lift up his fellow. But woe to him who is alone when he falls and has not another to lift him up! Again, if two lie together, they keep warm, but how can one keep warm alone? And though a man might prevail against one who is alone, two will withstand him—a threefold cord is not quickly broken.

Marriage is a serious and sacred union, but that does not mean we can't have fun together. Marriage expert Gary Thomas wrote a book years ago called *Sacred Marriage*. In it he asked the question, "What if God gave us marriage to make us holy more than happy?" Many read his question without reading the book and come to the wrong conclusion that happiness should not be a goal or it can't be a purpose in marriage. He didn't negate happiness as a possibility in marriage, but he did encourage readers to prioritize holiness over happiness.

Happiness and holiness are not at war with each other. Your spouse is your partner and companion through the grind of life. Why not have a little more fun through the grind? You don't need to choose between holiness and happiness. Go for both. Yes, life is hard, but that doesn't mean that marriage has to follow suit. It's time to lighten up, laugh, and enjoy one another more. You may be making marriage harder than it needs to be.

Yes, marriage can make us better, stronger, and holier, but it can also make us more content, protected, and joyful. Your companion is your spouse, not the grind of life. The enemy of your marriage is Satan, not your spouse. The source of life for your marriage is Jesus, not your spouse.

Settling the source issue is key to determining whether you are teammates or opponents. Have you or someone you know ever said something like the following?

"You complete me."
"I can't live without you."
"I'm lost without you."
"You are my world."

"I don't know what I would do without you."

"You are the air I breathe."

"Without you, life is meaningless."

"If we break up, I'll die."

"If I have you, I don't need anyone or anything else."

All of these statements take companionship too far. They cross the line of teammates and turn the spouse into a source. When your spouse becomes your source of life, you place expectations on him or her that God never intended.

If your spouse has become your source, start by firing your spouse. Do it right now.

Point to your spouse and say, "You're fired! You are no longer my source of life."

At the same time, fire yourself as the general manager of your spouse. This may feel like an elementary exercise, but decisions are powerful. Happy spouses plug into the true and only Source of life and spend their days giving the one they love the overflow.

2. Highly Happy Couples Resolve Anger Quickly and Avoid Throwing Things

Did your parents ever make you apologize to a sibling? Mine did. My first attempt at expressing remorse usually fell flat. So Mom and Dad made me repeat the performance. It always took me a few tries before the apology was believable. By *believable* I mean that I was able to convince my parents I felt sincere, but in reality, I wasn't. Despite my parents' best efforts, I went into marriage struggling with apologies. And I have a suspicion you did too.

For example, have you ever offered your spouse one of these apologies?

- "I'm sorry you feel that way."
- "If I offended you, I'm sorry."
- "If I hurt you, I'm sorry."
- "I'm sorry you took it that way."
- "I'm sorry I said it that way."

On paper and in list form, these apologies make me cringe. Why? Because they lack personal responsibility and point the finger of blame at the other person.

"I'm sorry you feel that way" is another way of saying, "You shouldn't feel that way." It's one of the world's worst apologies. You never need to apologize for another person's feelings because you're not responsible for them. You and I are responsible for our words and actions. The best apologies start with, "I'm sorry I said _____," and "I'm sorry I did _____." When you apologize for what you say and do, you are taking personal responsibility and saying to your spouse, "Your feelings matter." Bottom line: "You matter."

"If I offended you, I'm sorry" is another way of saying, "You shouldn't have been offended by that." Sometimes my joking can offend my wife. It better serves my marriage to apologize rather than saying, "I was kidding. Don't take it so seriously."

"If I hurt you, I'm sorry" is another way of saying, "You're being too sensitive." Again, you don't need to apologize for hurt feelings; you need to apologize for the words and actions that led to the hurt.

"I'm sorry you took it that way" is another way of saying, "That's not what I intended." Remember, what my spouse hears is more important than what I say. To honor your spouse, validate his or her feelings on the front end of the apology: "I can understand how that came across to you; please forgive my tone."

"I'm sorry I said it that way" is another way of saying, "What I said was right, but I said it in the wrong way," or "What I told you was truth and you needed to hear it, but maybe my tone wasn't right." If *probably* and *maybe* are ever in your apology, it's not a good apology. "Well, I *probably could* have said it better." No, you could have said it better. My approach, tone, and body language get me in way more trouble than my opinion or thoughts on an issue do.

A thriving marriage requires two spouses who are good at giving and receiving apologies. Ruth Bell Graham is known for saying, "A good marriage consists of two good forgivers."[1] A great marriage requires a husband and wife who are quick to apologize and quick to forgive. I know what you might be thinking:

- "I can't rush forgiveness."
- "I need time to process."

- "My heart is wounded, and I don't know how long it will take to heal."

I understand that sentiment, but I challenge the belief.

For the first half of our marriage, Amy and I had something called the "QMR" (Quarterly Marriage Realignment). We let things go and avoided conflict at all costs. One might call that sweeping it under the rug in hopes that it will go away. The problem is, it doesn't go away; it builds up. Then, like a volcano, the pressure is too much. For us, we went three months before eruption. Every couple is different. You may have an "MMR" (Monthly Marriage Realignment) or an "AMR" (Annual Marriage Realignment). Whatever your timeline, there's a better, biblical way.

Jesus calls it the "SMQ" (Settle Matters Quickly). He spoke these words in Matthew 5:25 when He said, "Come to terms quickly with your accuser while you are going with him to court." Don't let things drag out; deal with them. Amy and I now keep very short accounts. We prioritize fifteen to twenty minutes a day to ask about offenses, apologize if necessary, and forgive always.

Healing and forgiveness are different processes. Healing may take time, but forgiveness is immediate. Don't withhold forgiveness in an attempt to heal. Forgiveness is a first step toward healing. Forgive and allow God to heal you.

In Ephesians 4:31, the apostle Paul spells out clearly what we don't want building up inside of us: "Let all bitterness and wrath and anger and clamor and slander be put away from you, along with all malice." Christian or non-Christian, almost all would probably say, "Yeah, that shouldn't be a part of our lives. It harms us and destroys relationships."

"Be kind to one another, tenderhearted, forgiving one another, as God in Christ forgave you" (verse 32). You've heard it said, "forgive and forget," but Christians are called to forgive by taking it to the cross. Knowing we are forgiven by God gives us everything we need to forgive each other in marriage. The inability to forgive an apologizing spouse is a source problem, not a spouse problem. If I refuse my spouse's attempts at seeking forgiveness, that is between me and the Lord, not me and my spouse. I must forgive as a follower of Jesus, because I've been forgiven.

Gentle touch is a good way to assess where you are with your spouse. After conflict and reconciliation, a soft hand on the shoulder will tell you a lot. If the shoulder is pulled away, then there is still work to do. The heart is still closed. If the hand on the shoulder causes your spouse to turn toward you, then the heart is opening. I believe the same is true for humor and forgiveness. Kind, tenderhearted humor tells me often where I stand with Amy. Humor can be a great barometer for forgiveness. The key is to make the joke at my expense.

"I'm such an idiot."

"What was I thinking?"

"I know better."

Those statements, spoken in a tender tone with the proper timing and a little while after the offense, are usually met with a smile or a validating smirk. Making the joke at your spouse's expense is almost a guarantee for a setback.

I once heard a pastor encourage a couple to write down all of their offenses on a piece of paper then flush it down the toilet in an effort to forget them. I appreciate the heart behind the pastor's exhortation, but believe there is a much better way. I would encourage the couple to take the offenses and nail them to the cross. Reminders of a flushed offense or hurt are proof that it is not forgotten. Offenses and hurts left at the cross remind me they are forgiven.

When you say or do something that hurts your spouse, apologize for your words and actions. When your spouse apologizes, forgive "as God in Christ forgave you." Repeating these steps in marriage is key to a thriving marriage.

3. Highly Happy Couples Prioritize Quality Couple Time

At Date Night Comedy in Boulder, Colorado, I asked a couple, married sixty-three years, "What does it take to have a great marriage go sixty-three years?"

The husband said, "We go on two dates a week. She goes on Tuesday. I go on Thursday." Funny, but not the quality time we're talking about.

Amy and I love watching young couples on dates. From across the restaurant we watch as they get to know each other, raise eyebrows, and laugh at one another's stories. We love to guess how they met, how long they've been dating, and whether or not they are in it for the long haul.

More than watching young couples interact, we love watching senior couples laugh and enjoy life over their shared meal. When I say shared meal, I mean one entree and an extra plate. In Branson, Missouri, we minister to millions of tourists a year. The vast majority of those tourists are senior adults. Amy and I have plenty of opportunities to observe seniors. We love watching a couple well into their eighties roaring with laughter. They have walkers and canes because their bodies are haggard, but I can tell their marriage is not. We often comment, "Lord willing, if we make it to fifty or sixty years of marriage, we want to be the couple who howls with laughter as we help one another to our Buick." Our bodies will break down in the grind of life, but our marriage will not.

In my book *Fun Loving You*, I introduced the idea that a mentor shared with me early in ministry. Joe White, the president of Kanakuk Kamps, told me over breakfast one morning, "Your marriage needs a daily delay, a weekly withdrawal, and an annual abandon." All these years later, Amy and I still prioritize all three.

The daily delay is fifteen to twenty minutes a day of tech-free, child-free, distraction-free, face-to-face time. It keeps short accounts and allows for conversation on any topic necessary: budget, parenting, jobs, in-laws, household needs, dreaming, laughing, planning, or praying. Whatever you need, go with it.

There's a time and place for the daily delay, and it is different for every couple. Mornings work for some, while late evenings after the kids go to bed work for others. Many couples share with me that the moment of reconnection at the end of the workday is not the best time, since they are busy catching up on chores, playing with the kids, preparing supper, or simply unwinding from the day. Find a time that works for you both and make it a habit.

The high/low question is a great way to initiate the daily delay. Ask your spouse, "What were the high and low of your day?" It digs a little deeper than, "How was your day?" And it doesn't allow for a "Fine" answer.

The weekly withdrawal is your date night. Schedule and protect it at all costs. Keep it fun and light. It is your time as a couple to de-stress and pursue romance and intimacy. The daily delay protects your date night from serious conversations. Nothing sucks the life out of the weekly withdrawal faster than a heated discussion about spending or a long discussion about the kids.

Every time you go on a date, you tell your kids, family, and friends, "Our marriage is important." However, quality couple time evades many couples who get stuck in the rut of "dinner and a movie." If your marriage lacks creativity in the dating department, try something new immediately. Consider roller-skating, cooking classes, spelunking, water skiing, zip-lining, fishing, bowling, or hiking. There are even online dating sites like getdatebox.com that will mail you each month "everything you need for a fun and creative date." Novelty is a key to creating great dates worth repeating.

The three primary objections to date night are:

"We have no time."

"We have no money."

"We have kids."

There's a solution for all three. Dates don't require a ton of time to plan, you don't need to spend big bucks, and you can find folks to watch the kids. If you can't afford a babysitter, consider asking grandparents or friends. Kid swap with another couple. You take the kids for their Tuesday night date, and they take yours for Thursday night.

The annual abandon is modeled for us by the Shulammite bride and Solomon. She invites her shepherd king out of town on a passionate, romantic getaway:

I am my beloved's,
    and his desire is for me.
Come, my beloved,
    let us go out into the fields
    and lodge in the villages;
let us go out early to the vineyards
    and see whether the vines have budded,
whether the grape blossoms have opened
    and the pomegranates are in bloom.
There I will give you my love.
The mandrakes give forth fragrance,
    and beside our doors are all choice fruits,

new as well as old,
which I have laid up for you, O my beloved.
SONG OF SOLOMON 7:10-13

"There I will give you my love" is her way of saying, "I want you." An annual abandon creates anticipation in marriage. If you plan one, you have something on the calendar to look forward to for weeks and months leading up to it. The annual abandon gets you out of the house and out of town. It breaks the routine of the ordinary week. Out-of-town getaways that include play, laughter, dreaming, and adventure keep your marriage from being consumed by the power of ordinary.

One final consideration for the weekly withdrawal and annual abandon that you may initially oppose, but give it some thought: As you work on your family's budget, add a line item called "couple fun," "marital satisfaction," or "one fun marriage." Investing in your marriage is as important as your child's education and your retirement plan.

I often hear couples say, "We can't afford to take vacations away from the kids." But vacations need not be outrageously expensive. You don't need a yacht to enjoy time on the water and you don't need a five-star hotel to enjoy a romantic vacation. However, spoiling your spouse every now and then is not a waste of money, and it is more affordable than you think. Consider all of your expenses while finding the funds to invest in your marriage. That might mean buying a used vehicle rather than a new one. Eat out with the kids less and with each other more. Some couples choose to buy a smaller house with a smaller mortgage so they can do more together.

These ideas may seem drastic, or perhaps ridiculous. However, your marriage is worth it. Your children need a mom and dad who invest relationally, emotionally, physically, and yes, even financially, in their marriage. Don't go into debt for the sake of your marriage, but don't give up on some great experiences together because of other stuff in life. Invest in experiences, not stuff.

Amy and I drove our family minivan to over 206,000 miles on the odometer. When people asked, "Ted, when are you going to get a new car?" I responded with, "I'm driving this one until the wheels fall off because I love dating my wife." When we finally bought a new car, the dealer did a walk around the old minivan and said, "We don't want it, but if it means you won't buy a car from us I'll give you five hundred dollars." I said, "No thanks, we'll donate it to a ministry." Our van was on its last legs, but our marriage is not.

4. Highly Happy Couples Speak Words of High Value in Private and Public

Confirmation bias describes what happens when we make a decision and then look for the evidence to back up our decision. This happens in marriage when we assign negative feelings to our spouse's words and actions.

For example, she says . . .

"**He's so lazy!**" If you have decided that your husband is lazy, you will look for the evidence to back that up and only see him napping on the couch, or forgetting the household chores, and not see him working ten hours a day.

Or he says . . .

"**She's such a nag!**" If you decide your wife is a nag, you will hear words out of her mouth in a nagging tone. You won't notice the neutral or tender words that might be spoken throughout the day. She says, "It's time for dinner," and he's thinking, *Dang! She's constantly on me!*

That's confirmation bias at work in the negative, but it can also be used to fuel that which honors your spouse. Honor esteems your spouse as highly valuable.

In Philippians 4:8 the author not only tells those who follow Jesus to be careful about their thoughts but he gets very specific on how they should choose to think. He wrote, "Finally, brothers, whatever is true, whatever is honorable, whatever is just, whatever is pure, whatever is lovely, whatever is commendable, if there is any excellence, if there is anything worthy of praise, think about these things."

Choose a word from that list that describes your spouse's attitude and share it with your spouse. Explain how he or she embodies that word. I've seen it time and time again. Spoken words that are true, honorable, just, pure, lovely, commendable, excellent, and praiseworthy almost always bring a smile to your spouse's face. If you do this often, the smile quickly turns to blushing, giggles, and if you don't let up, the out-loud laugh. Honor and laughter go good together.

One of the ways to begin to develop the habit of thinking more honorable thoughts about your spouse is to actually begin making a list of all his or her honorable traits. Amy and I keep honor lists on each other and they are constantly growing. Here is a fill-in-the-blank list to get you started. When I say "get you started," the hope is that you will add to this list as the years go by.

Reasons why _____ is highly valuable.
(insert spouse's name)

1. Your greatest strength is revealed when you _____
_____
_____.

2. The way you treat others encourages me to _____
_____
_____.

3. You are at your best when you _____
_____
_____.

4. One of the reasons I fell in love with you and still love you is _____ _____
_____.

5. I love it when you say, "_____
_____ _____
_____."

6. I admire the fact that you never get mad when _____
_____ _____
_____.

7. You laugh every time when _____
_____ _____
_____.

8. The older you get the better _____
_____ _____
_____.

9. You are extremely patient with _____
_____ _____
_____.

10. It's cute the way you _____
_____ _____
_____.

What should you do with this list? First of all, keep it handy. When you experience conflict in your marriage, refer back to it and remind yourself of the decisions you made. Don't edit the list; add to it. Spend your days looking for the evidence to validate your claims.

Second, read it out loud to your spouse. Spoken words of high value are greater than written words because you get more feeling out of it. If the majority of communication is nonverbal, then you want your spouse to hear your tone and see your posture. I dare you to not get choked up while reading the list.

Finally, read the list out loud over your spouse in front of family and friends. The Shulammite woman referred to this as "his banner over me is love" (Song of Solomon 2:4, NASB). Be known as a safe couple who speak words of praise over one another. Birthdays, anniversaries, and holidays are a great time to pull out the honor list and let everyone know of your love for each other. Our family so cherishes honor that we keep lists on our children and parents too. Forget the Hallmark cards. Honor lists are better.

Nothing grieves me more than to see a married couple running each other down. I sometimes want to approach them and ask, "You do know you're in public and others can hear you, right?" Every time I see it, I thank Amy for her kindness in public and private.

Thank you for not scolding me.

Thank you for not talking down to me.

Thank you for not bossing me around.

Thank you for not correcting me when I speak to others.

Thank you for not telling me to "shut up."

A Final Thought on Habits

As a pastor I meet unhappy couples a lot. In talking with other pastors, I've discovered that there are two ways we respond to unhappy couples. As mentioned earlier, some pastors validate the unhappy couple by saying things like, "Well, marriage isn't about your happiness anyway," or "The goal of marriage is not happiness." Again, this response has become a theme for many counseling sessions and sermon series, but I don't think it is a helpful response. It's become the knee-jerk reaction of many church leaders.

What is a couple supposed to do with that? "Oh honey, I guess our marriage isn't as bad as we thought. Pastor says we're not supposed to be happy."

There's a better way, and it leads to a high level of marital satisfaction. Enjoying life together is a by-product of good choices. Let's start by telling the unhappy couple that joy in marriage is not only possible but it is also God's desire for them. Let's start by committing to get on the same page as teammates. With that comes the commitment to resolve anger and keep short accounts. That will begin to open us up and create a longing to spend quality time together. It will be desired, not forced. And finally, words of high value will be the icing on the cake. Get these four habits into your marriage and the fun and laughter will be there with you hand in hand.

Your Laughter Score

For a possible 20,000 points,

1. Lightning Round. Word associations spark fast fun, since they don't allow you to think about your answer. It is a quick revealer of the heart. With a lighthearted, fast pace, ask your spouse to choose between the two of you on the following questions. Allow for disagreement and a little friendly competition because therein lie the outbursts of laughter.

1. Most athletic?
2. Most romantic?
3. Most talkative?
4. Most argumentative?
5. Most aggressive driver?
6. Best singer?
7. Best driver?
8. Best dancer?
9. Biggest spender?
10. Quickest to forgive?

My attempt at humor . . .

Fell flat .... 0 points
Made my spouse smirk .... 1,000 points
Made my spouse smile .... 2,000 points

Made my spouse snicker.............................3,000 points
Made my spouse giggle...............................4,000 points
Made my spouse chuckle............................5,000 points
Made my spouse cackle ....6,000 points
Made my spouse belly laugh.......................7,000 points
Made my spouse howl ....8,000 points
Made my spouse shriek ....9,000 points
Made my spouse die laughing..................10,000 points

_____ Her Score _____ His Score

The next time I attempt this humor, I will

_____

2. Would You Rather. Ask each question out loud, and each of you gives an immediate response. You don't need to rush through it as fast as you did the Lightning Round. Leave room for banter.

1. Would you rather vacation in New York City or Miami, Florida?
2. Would you rather receive $5,000 a month for the rest of your life or a check for $1,000,000?
3. Would you rather be in a movie or full season of a sitcom?
4. Would you rather live in a tiny house or an RV?
5. Would you rather live without Wi-Fi or television?

6. Would you rather live without your mobile phone or car?
7. Would you rather dissect a frog or a turtle?
8. Would you rather spend a night in the White House or Buckingham Palace?
9. Would you rather be Ironman or the Hulk?
10. Would you rather do 500 jumping jacks or 50 push-ups?

My attempt at humor . . .

Fell flat .... 0 points
Made my spouse smirk .... 1,000 points
Made my spouse smile .... 2,000 points
Made my spouse snicker .... 3,000 points
Made my spouse giggle .... 4,000 points
Made my spouse chuckle .... 5,000 points
Made my spouse cackle .... 6,000 points
Made my spouse belly laugh .... 7,000 points
Made my spouse howl .... 8,000 points
Made my spouse shriek .... 9,000 points
Made my spouse die laughing .... 10,000 points

_____ Her Score   _____ His Score

The next time I attempt this humor, I will

_____

Write your scores on page 206, too.

Conversation Starters and a Few More Laughs

- If your small group is going through *A Love That Laughs* together, take a few minutes to share words of honor over your spouse in front of the group.

- Who do you need to forgive?

- If you had unlimited resources, where would you go on your annual abandon? How are you getting there? What activities will you schedule? How long would you stay? How much lovemaking will there be? Any creative ideas for romance?

- What can you do this week to prioritize your marriage in the home?

CHAPTER 8

Don't Get a Divorce, Get a Donut

So they are no longer two but one flesh. What therefore
God has joined together, let not man separate.

MATTHEW 19:6

———————

With mirth and laughter let old wrinkles come.

WILLIAM SHAKESPEARE

I BELIEVE DONUTS lower your risk of divorce. Through personal experience, I know it is impossible to fight while eating a donut. In twenty-three years of marriage, Amy and I have never once fought while eating sweets. I challenge you to try it.

This is marriage advice I follow faithfully because it's backed by real research. One study shows that a marriage where the husband has a higher BMI (Body Mass Index) than the wife has a lower risk of divorce.[1] I like to remind Amy that every time I eat a donut I am lowering our risk of divorce.

My love of sugary snacks makes it tough to preach in

skinny jeans, but it helps my marriage. I own one pair of skinny jeans that you will never see me wearing. They're my little treat for Amy.

At a recent comedy show, my comedian friend Paul Harris asked a couple married seventy years, "What does it take to have a marriage last seventy years?"

The old man yelled to the stage, "Don't die!"

That is beautiful!

Seriously, what does it take, besides staying alive, to have a thriving marriage in which a husband and wife enjoy life together?

For some couples, the idea of laughing together and enjoying one another really does seem like an impossible dream. The grind of life has worn them down to the point that they're experiencing real pain and real trouble.

I truly believe that laughter is a fantastic tool for building a happier marriage and a happier life, but you may need a little help getting to the point where you can begin to bring joy back into your relationship with your spouse.

Through laughter and some "aha" moments in this book, you may now be ready to ask some deeper questions. This is not at all disconnected from the theme of this book, but serves as a firm foundation to the theme. Your joy has a source, and His name is Jesus. By deepening your commitment to Jesus and to your marriage, you can find a pathway back to joy.

If your marriage is having a hard time breathing, it's time to start hoping.

There Is Hope

If you've been thinking, *I don't think our marriage will ever be fun* or *We may share a few laughs, but not to the level encouraged in this book*, I want to encourage you. I believe you can experience levels of marital satisfaction that you've never dreamed possible. More than dreaming, I want you to start hoping.

"If you're breathing, you have hope." That is a core value at Woodland Hills Family Church, and you hear it from the pulpit often. Ecclesiastes 9:4 says, "But he who is joined with all the living has hope." We believe Jesus breathes life into dead souls, marriages, and families. Never bet against hope.

In Revelation 2, Jesus shares with the church at Ephesus their need for a reset:

> I know your works, your toil and your patient
> endurance, and how you cannot bear with those who
> are evil, but have tested those who call themselves
> apostles and are not, and found them to be false. I
> know you are enduring patiently and bearing up for
> my name's sake, and you have not grown weary. But
> I have this against you, that you have abandoned the
> love you had at first.
>
> REVELATION 2:2-4

Jesus commends the church at Ephesus for what they are doing well, but then calls out the fact that they are going through the motions. They have forgotten their first love. Jesus is the source of everything we do. Christians and churches often start strong in their love for the Lord, but then drift away from the source while continuing to do great deeds.

Maybe your marriage is in the same spot. You are going through the right motions, but your love and passion for one another wanes. The fire, joy, and excitement you once had are no longer there. You've excused it because of the years, your age, or life getting the best of you.

Do you want it back? If the flame is out or barely flickering, do you want a blazing fire again? It doesn't matter how you met, how long you've been married, or how you've treated one another up until now, you can have a thriving marriage starting this very moment.

Written in 1834, one of my favorite hymns is "My Hope Is Built on Nothing Less." I learned these words as a small child and they stay with me over forty years later:

My hope is built on nothing less
Than Jesus' blood and righteousness;
I dare not trust the sweetest frame,
But wholly lean on Jesus' name.

On Christ, the solid Rock, I stand;
All other ground is sinking sand,
All other ground is sinking sand.[2]

When I sing these words, I meditate on the words of Jesus in Matthew 7:24-27:

> Everyone then who hears these words of mine and
> does them will be like a wise man who built his
> house on the rock. And the rain fell, and the floods
> came, and the winds blew and beat on that house,
> but it did not fall, because it had been founded on
> the rock. And everyone who hears these words of
> mine and does not do them will be like a foolish
> man who built his house on sand. And the rain fell,
> and the floods came, and the winds blew and beat
> against that house, and it fell, and great was the
> fall of it.

A life and marriage built on the solid rock of Christ Jesus withstands the rain, floods, and wind. A life and marriage built on the sand experiences a "great crash" when faced with the same elements.

When a marriage crashes, a couple may say, "No one knows what I'm going through." But what if they do?

All couples experience rain, floods, and wind, but not all couples have the same foundation. Your foundation determines your ability to withstand what comes at you. Most crashing couples I counsel have built their marriage on sand.

I often get messages from folks that read something like this, "We haven't been in church for a while and we know we need to get back. Some things have come up in my life and I need to talk to someone about it." I've found that such messages come from couples who drift from the church and their faith, and then are stuck wondering what happened to their marriage.

The wind, rain, and floods of bankruptcy, health problems, conflict, job loss, a new baby, a rebellious teenager, mental health issues, or family dysfunction hit their marriage. Their foundation is not secure, and they are headed for a great crash. We plug them in by encouraging growth through reading of Scripture, regular worship, fellowship with other believers, and serving others. Throughout this process of getting their life and marriage back on the rock of Christ Jesus, I remind them, "If you found help in the local church when your life was falling apart, stay put. It may keep your life from falling apart again."

The prophet Jeremiah echoes this teaching:

Blessed is the man who trusts in the LORD,
    whose trust is the LORD.
He is like a tree planted by water,
    that sends out its roots by the stream,
and does not fear when heat comes,
    for its leaves remain green,
and is not anxious in the year of drought,
    for it does not cease to bear fruit.

JEREMIAH 17:7-8

Jesus gives the church at Ephesus, and you and me, a clear path back to our first love:

> Remember therefore from where you have fallen; repent, and do the works you did at first. If not, I will come to you and remove your lampstand from its place, unless you repent.
>
> REVELATION 2:5

It's as direct as consider, repent, and redo.

Consider: Where Is Your Marriage Now?

I first drew the following illustration on a whiteboard at our church. I simply asked our congregation, "Are you deciding your way into marital satisfaction or are you drifting away from it?"

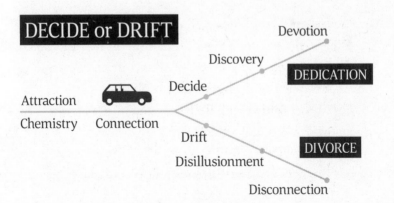

Almost every romantic relationship starts the same way, but there's a fork in the road and you must choose between decision or drift. Dedication or divorce. You either decide your way into marital satisfaction, or you avoid decisions and drift. When does drift begin? Marital drift begins the day you stop deciding.

Happily married couples and divorced couples score similarly on *relational satisfaction* at the beginning of the marriage. No matter how you met or how long you dated, early in relationship formation you enjoyed being with one another. Yes, there are exceptions to this, but the vast majority of couples come together because of attraction and chemistry. They are physically attracted to one another and enjoy spending quality time together.

While attraction looks similar for most couples, connection looks different for each couple. Some are attracted to one another and go with hookup and cohabitation. That is the beginning of their drift. They're not making decisions, they're letting things happen. They're "seeing where it goes."

Others choose connection in the form of marriage. They make the decision, "For better or worse, in sickness and in health, for richer or for poorer, till death do us part."

For those who honor marriage and the marriage bed (Hebrews 13:4), they decide their way into a season of discovery. Whereas chemistry is a period of highlighting similarities and downplaying differences, discovery moves beyond similarities and explores the differences. Moving through the discovery of differences with enthusiasm to learn about your spouse is called devotion. You have a strong desire to get to know one another, and when you learn something new there is curiosity and fascination, not disappointment and frustration.

Couples in drift grow disillusioned with unmet expectations. The gap between our expectations and reality causes stress, which in these situations is a socially acceptable term for anger. We are mad that we are not getting what we expected.

Disillusionment moves us to disconnection. You stay married, but there is no physical intimacy. One spouse may even move out of the bedroom into another room down the hall or downstairs. Unchecked, disconnection explores other options such as separation and divorce.

Considering where your marriage is right now means you look back to moments when you drifted. Some couples drift after the birth of a child. Others drift while trying to conceive a child. A move across the country or taking a new job may cause a spouse to focus solely on their work and neglect the marriage.

In the book *Mission Drift*, author Peter Greer shares how nonprofits and parachurch ministries can drift from their original mission. He shares two examples that really hit home for me. The first is a university mission statement that reads, "To be plainly instructed and consider well that the main end of your life and studies is to know God and Jesus Christ."[3] That is the original intent of Harvard University, founded in 1636.

Here's another example: George Williams started a Bible study in 1844 for displaced young men on the streets of London. These Bible studies eventually became a movement known as the Young Men's Christian Association (YMCA).

One hundred and seventy-five years later, your town may have a fitness center called The Y, with the "Christian" mission downplayed or missing altogether.

Mission drift occurs when donor dollars have strings attached. Other times it is leaders, presidents, and board members that take it off course. Drift doesn't happen overnight. Subtle changes, that may seem harmless at the time, place the organization in drift over a long period of time.

Like organizations that don't remain diligent, marriages drift when husbands and wives stop deciding their way into marital satisfaction. Couples allow unmet expectations and unresolved conflict around money to take them off course. Others drift when their first child is born and they stop dating. Maybe you've experienced the voices of a parent, in-law, friend, sibling, or coworker bringing doubt and drift to your marriage. Or was it your drifting from the cross that caused your marriage to suffer? For many couples, marital drift can be traced back to the moment when one or both drifted in their relationship with the Lord.

Whatever the case, there is good news: Drift does not need to be the beginning of the end for a marriage.

Repent: What Do You Need to Confess?

When you call out your drift, you bring it into the light. Confess it before God and each other.

And again, remember that seeking forgiveness is not the same as healing. Don't demand forgiveness; ask for it. Don't withhold forgiveness; give it freely. Forgive the sin of your spouse, and trust God to bring your healing. Forgiveness is a decision; healing is a process.

Healing takes time. As you look at what you need to redo in your marriage, you may need some more time with some of these, especially physical intimacy.

Redo: What Do You Need to Start Doing Again?

Marital satisfaction depends on factors and skills that couples and spouses can do something about in any season or stage of life. You practiced these skills as daters and newlyweds. Which ones will you return to immediately? Which ones will take some more time? Here are five factors and skills most couples practice early in marriage. For most, these were as easy as breathing.

1. You couldn't stop thinking of each other. The Shulammite woman said of Solomon, "My beloved is to me a sachet of myrrh that lies between my breasts" (Song of Solomon 1:13). In that day, a sachet of myrrh scented the body. The thought of Solomon lingered with her wherever she went and all throughout the day.

Here's how Amy and I ended phone calls while dating:

"No, you hang up first."

"No, you hang up first."

"I'm not getting off the phone until you do."

"I'm never hanging up."

Twenty-three years later, my wife still has me in her thoughts constantly. No lie. She does nothing without thinking about my needs as well. When she gets up to get water, she always asks, "Do you need a glass of water?"

"Thank you, yes," I say.

On more than one occasion, I've waited thirty minutes for the water and it never arrived. You know why? Amy started a project on her way to get it. My wife has 2.4 million thoughts going through her brain at any given time.

After thirty minutes of no water, I try to sneak to the refrigerator to get it and I see her on a ladder painting a wall in our bedroom. What? I didn't even know we bought paint or discussed painting.

When she hears the water dispenser on the fridge, she yells from the ladder, "I was still getting that." She never forgets, but she has a lot to do.

Return to the simple task of thinking about your spouse as you go throughout your day.

2. You anticipated intimacy. You looked forward to being together physically and it consumed your thoughts. The Shulammite woman, while dating Solomon, anticipated physical intimacy within marriage: "Draw me after you; let us run. The king has brought me into his chambers" (Song of Solomon 1:4). *Boom-boom-chicky-chicky-boom-boom.*

A few years ago at church I encouraged the women to go home and shove their husband onto the bed at some point during the week. That request shocked our congregation, but many took me up on it.

The next Sunday, one guy came up to me and said, "Pastor, do you mind finishing that teaching from last week?" I had no idea what he was talking about.

He said, "My wife pushed me onto the bed three times this week and then walked right out of the room each time."

That's not at all what I intended.

3. You complimented one another often. Remember when you looked for the best in each other and stated it? Solomon complimented the Shulammite woman when he said to her,

> How beautiful you are, my darling,
> How beautiful you are!
> Your eyes are like doves.
> SONG OF SOLOMON 1:15, NASB

She complimented him by saying,

> How handsome you are, my beloved,
> And so pleasant!
> Indeed, our couch is luxuriant!
> SONG OF SOLOMON 1:16, NASB

Simple and short compliments are powerful when they are sincere and frequent. This was easy when you first dated. Try leaving an encouraging note on the mirror in the morning.

Slip a Post-it note on her purse before she walks out the door. And by all means, text! A one-line, flirty text with some heart emojis goes a long way.

4. You praised each other in public. Not only did you compliment often, you spoke highly of one another to strangers, friends, and family. You were delighted to be a couple. You wanted everyone to know you were together. You pointed out the best in each other.

The Shulammite referred to this as a banner: "He has brought me to his banquet hall, and his banner over me is love" (2:4, NASB). In other words, she found safety and security when she was with him. Like an army, they were together fighting for the same purpose and cause.

5. You eliminated potential threats to your marriage. You didn't flirt around with anyone or anything that led you toward drift. Like Solomon and the Shulammite, you chased them off:

> Catch the foxes for us,
>   the little foxes
> that spoil the vineyards,
>   for our vineyards are in blossom.
> SONG OF SOLOMON 2:15

Your marriage is a vineyard in bloom. It needs time and protection to reach harvest. In Solomon's day, stone walls protected the vineyard. It was easy to keep out the big foxes, but it took time walking around the wall looking for small holes or gaps in the gate that allowed the small foxes in. Over time, little foxes ate away at the vineyard if the vintner was not paying close attention. Don't allow the little foxes to destroy your budding love. Don't allow the foxes to destroy your fun and laughs. Chase them out. The marriage that laughs lasts.

My wife is a romantic. She wants us to die when we are old, in bed, holding hands, and facing each other, like the couple in the movie *The Notebook*.

I told her, "For that to happen you will need to take some serious steps toward sabotaging your health. The next time we go to Cracker Barrel, I need you to join me, not judge me, when I order chicken-fried steak. And for the health of our marriage, I'd like to take you to Dunkin' Donuts for breakfast tomorrow morning."

Your Laughter Score

For a possible 20,000 points,

1. Shove Him onto the Bed. This can be planned or unexpected. Talking about it may get you some points. This is a timed challenge. Give yourself a week. How many times can you push him down in a week? Keep it playful and safe. We don't need either one of you getting hurt. Your facial expressions will communicate your intentions more than the strength in the shove. If this is a puzzling activity to you, you may need to go back to pages 180–181, read the advice I gave to my congregation, and read between the lines.

My attempt at humor . . .

Fell flat ....0 points
Made my spouse smirk .... 1,000 points
Made my spouse smile .... 2,000 points
Made my spouse snicker .... 3,000 points
Made my spouse giggle .... 4,000 points
Made my spouse chuckle .... 5,000 points
Made my spouse cackle .... 6,000 points
Made my spouse belly laugh .... 7,000 points
Made my spouse howl .... 8,000 points
Made my spouse shriek .... 9,000 points
Made my spouse die laughing .... 10,000 points

_____ Her Score _____ His Score

The next time I attempt this humor, I will

_____

2. Carry Her across the Threshold. If you have physical challenges with this one, get creative. Use an office chair with wheels. Make it a short walk. Pick her up at the bedside and gently lay her down. When I told Amy I was going to do this, she shrieked. That's 9,000 points without exerting myself. It's getting easier and easier.

My attempt at humor . . .

Fell flat..0 points
Made my spouse smirk............................... 1,000 points
Made my spouse smile.................................2,000 points
Made my spouse snicker..............................3,000 points
Made my spouse giggle................................4,000 points
Made my spouse chuckle.............................5,000 points
Made my spouse cackle ....6,000 points
Made my spouse belly laugh........................7,000 points
Made my spouse howl..................................8,000 points
Made my spouse shriek ....9,000 points
Made my spouse die laughing................. 10,000 points

_____ Her Score _____ His Score

The next time I attempt this humor, I will

_____

Write your scores on page 206, too.

Conversation Starters and a Few More Laughs

- What candy best describes your wedding night?

    A. Hot Tamales
    B. Fast Break
    C. Good & Plenty
    D. Snickers

- Share a few activities you loved while dating that you wish you'd get back to.

- Are you committed to Scripture as the driver of your marriage? Would you be open to reading the Bible together?

- What foxes do you need to chase from your marriage vineyard?

CHAPTER 9

Extra Credit

*Ten Fast, Easy, and Free Ways
to Make Your Spouse Laugh*

TOURING THE CASTLES of Ireland.

Walking through vineyards in northern France.

Photographing lions on an African safari.

Backpacking and fly-fishing in Alaska.

Amy and I have done none of the above, but we dream about each one. We may never go on any of those trips, but why should that stop us from reaping the benefits of planning them? The sights, smells, tastes, and sounds of those places intrigue us. Perusing travel magazines and dreaming is life-giving for us.

The same is true for laughter. You may not do some of the activities in this chapter, but that shouldn't stop you from talking about them. Amy and I have not done all of the activities in this book, but we've laughed over each one. As I shared a few with friends and family, they laughed over the thought of them. Remember, laughter starts in the mind.

Also, the timing may not be right for you and some of these activities. You may need to store them away and let them hit you in the moment years from now. Some of the more intimate activities require exact timing. If done at the wrong time or in the wrong place, you might get arrested. You'll soon see what I mean.

This chapter alone has 100,000 possible points to earn. Some will be no-brainers, and you'll say, "No way!" to others. Whether you do the activity or not, score the laughs and "work" on your shared sense of humor. *Record your scores on Your Final Laughter Score.*

1. Kids Say the Darnedest Things. Children are a great source of comedy in the home. My mom remembers everything funny I ever said and shares it at family gatherings every chance she gets. That got me thinking. We should journal what our kids say because they give us so much great material. Share a few of your favorite moments or comments from your kids. Share it with sound effects and physical humor. Here are a few from moms I know. Read through them to jostle your own memory. Laughs while reading through these count toward your score.[1]

A mom was teaching her son how to give people compliments. He took her instruction and complimented the first person he saw, which happened to be a cashier. He said, "You have very nice bags, ma'am."

One mom knew her shopping addiction was a problem when she shared with her son, "I had a terrible day at work." Attempting to comfort his mom, the son replied, "Mom, do you need to go to Walmart?"

A little boy was constipated and screamed to his mom from the bathroom, "Mom, get the OxiClean—it gets out the tough stuff."

A mom confronted her daughter when she caught her with an empty candy-bar wrapper and chocolate all over her mouth. All the little girl said was, "Sorry, Mom, my blood sugar was low."

A dad was in the driveway siphoning gas from the car the old fashioned way. He had a hose snaked into the car's tank and sucked it out with his mouth. When some got in his mouth, he had to spit it out. His son saw this and said to the mom, "When I get married, I'm gonna have my wife do that."

Marcia confessed to me that she didn't know what was worse, her daughter eating a sandwich that had been in a shoe for two weeks or the fact that as her mom she didn't care and let her eat it.

A father and son shopped for the new family car. When they got home, the son announced to his mom, "Dad decided that he wants an STD."

While watching a special on the Discovery Channel with the whole family, a Cialis commercial came on at the break. After the term "E.D." was mentioned for the fifth time, the kindergartner announced to his parents, "Oh yeah, two kids in my class struggle with that. They go to the nurse's office every day to get pills for it." Shocked, the parents explained, "No son, that's A.D.D."

A four-year-old sketched out a picture of God and the teacher said, "Oh honey, no one knows what God looks like." The little girl answered, "They will when I'm done."

Most of my congregational prayers end with, "And everyone agreed and said . . ." After hearing that for years, one girl in our congregation ended her family's meal prayer with, "And everyone agreed with Ted and said . . ."

My attempt at humor . . .

Fell flat .... 0 points
Made my spouse smirk .... 1,000 points
Made my spouse smile .... 2,000 points
Made my spouse snicker .... 3,000 points
Made my spouse giggle .... 4,000 points
Made my spouse chuckle .... 5,000 points
Made my spouse cackle .... 6,000 points
Made my spouse belly laugh .... 7,000 points
Made my spouse howl .... 8,000 points
Made my spouse shriek .... 9,000 points
Made my spouse die laughing .... 10,000 points

_____ Her Score _____ His Score

2. Dream a Little Dream with Me. Take turns dreaming. Use one of the following conversation starters or think of your own. Whatever your spouse shares, you must respond with, "I can see you doing that." Consider answering these opposite your bent and personality. Give answers your spouse knows don't fit you.

If I had an unlimited budget for a vacation, I would

_____

_____ .

If they made a movie about my life and I could choose which actor played my part, I would definitely choose _____.

If could live in a foreign country for a year, I would choose _____ because _____.

If I could eat only one dessert for the rest of my life, it would be _____.

My attempt at humor . . .

Fell flat...0 points
Made my spouse smirk............................ 1,000 points
Made my spouse smile.............................2,000 points
Made my spouse snicker...........................3,000 points
Made my spouse giggle.............................4,000 points
Made my spouse chuckle..........................5,000 points
Made my spouse cackle ....6,000 points
Made my spouse belly laugh......................7,000 points
Made my spouse howl...............................8,000 points
Made my spouse shriek ....9,000 points
Made my spouse die laughing.................. 10,000 points

_____ Her Score _____ His Score

3. Sixty-Second Calorie Burn. This is an invigorating activity that you can challenge each other with in public or private.

With your smart watches set, track how many calories you each burn in sixty seconds. Jumping jacks, wind sprints, push-ups, and sit-ups all work. The only thing you can't do is stand there and shake your fist to trick the watch. If only one spouse has a watch, take turns using it. If your only smart device is your phone, that works too.

My attempt at humor . . .

Fell flat... 0 points
Made my spouse smirk............................. 1,000 points
Made my spouse smile.............................. 2,000 points
Made my spouse snicker............................ 3,000 points
Made my spouse giggle............................. 4,000 points
Made my spouse chuckle........................... 5,000 points
Made my spouse cackle .... 6,000 points
Made my spouse belly laugh...................... 7,000 points
Made my spouse howl .... 8,000 points
Made my spouse shriek .... 9,000 points
Made my spouse die laughing................... 10,000 points

_____ Her Score _____ His Score

4. When Was the First Time You Remember . . . Amy and I are shocked that after twenty-three years of marriage, there are still stories from childhood that have never been told. Someone will say something that recalls a story one of us forgot about. I'm sure you also have some untold stories. Here are some questions to get you started.

When was the first time you remember hearing laughter?
When was the first time you remember feeling excited?
When was the first time you remember getting lost?
When was the first time you remember being frightened?
When was the first time you remember being left alone?
When was the first time you remember helping someone who was hurt?

My attempt at humor . . .

Fell flat .... 0 points
Made my spouse smirk .... 1,000 points
Made my spouse smile .... 2,000 points
Made my spouse snicker .... 3,000 points
Made my spouse giggle .... 4,000 points
Made my spouse chuckle .... 5,000 points
Made my spouse cackle .... 6,000 points
Made my spouse belly laugh .... 7,000 points
Made my spouse howl .... 8,000 points
Made my spouse shriek .... 9,000 points
Made my spouse die laughing .... 10,000 points

_____ Her Score _____ His Score

5. Sixty Seconds of NSTs. An NST is a non-sexual touch. We shoot for a minimum of twelve NSTs in our marriage a day. The goal of an NST is not sex. Here is a starter list to get the ball rolling. See how many you can get in within sixty seconds:

1. Hold hands
2. Kiss cheek or forehead
3. Forehead to forehead
4. Hug
5. Scratch back
6. Hand on thigh
7. Hand on small of back
8. Hand to face
9. Massage shoulders and neck
10. Rub feet
11. Playful tap
12. Brush hair over ear

My attempt at humor . . .

Fell flat...0 points
Made my spouse smirk.............................1,000 points
Made my spouse smile..............................2,000 points
Made my spouse snicker...........................3,000 points
Made my spouse giggle............................4,000 points
Made my spouse chuckle..........................5,000 points

Made my spouse cackle ....6,000 points
Made my spouse belly laugh.......................7,000 points
Made my spouse howl ....8,000 points
Made my spouse shriek ....9,000 points
Made my spouse die laughing...................10,000 points

_____ Her Score _____ His Score

6. Lovemaking Playlist. The first time I encouraged couples to create a lovemaking playlist is when iPods were the new thing and docking stations were the rage. At one of Gary Smalley's conferences, I shared with the crowd the need for this and a docking station. At the end of the session, a senior woman approached Gary and told him it was totally inappropriate for Ted to be discussing things of this nature in church. I came in halfway through the conversation. She misunderstood and had no idea what a docking station was. She thought it was a device to enhance lovemaking. I had to tell her, "It's basically a radio!" Spend a few minutes discussing which songs should go on the playlist and why. Again, throw in some unexpected suggestions for shock.

My attempt at humor . . .

Fell flat...0 points
Made my spouse smirk ....1,000 points

Made my spouse smile..................................2,000 points

Made my spouse snicker.............................3,000 points

Made my spouse giggle..............................4,000 points

Made my spouse chuckle...........................5,000 points

Made my spouse cackle ....6,000 points

Made my spouse belly laugh.......................7,000 points

Made my spouse howl................................8,000 points

Made my spouse shriek ....9,000 points

Made my spouse die laughing..................10,000 points

_____ Her Score _____ His Score

7. The Crockpot Candle. When it comes to sexual intimacy, as someone has said, men are microwaves and women are crockpots. If you want to enjoy a nice meal when you get home, you need to turn it on before you leave the house. Declare a candle in your house (it can be any candle) "The Crockpot Candle." When it's lit, it means, "Tonight's the night." Light it in the morning before you leave for work and enjoy a day of flirting with one another—just be sure to blow the candle out before you leave the house; you want to send a message to your spouse, not the fire department. Send emails and texts with the lit emoji. Increase the nonsexual touching leading up to the night. *Warning:* Be careful of attitudes, actions, and words that might get the candle blown out during the day.

My attempt at humor . . .

Fell flat .... 0 points
Made my spouse smirk .... 1,000 points
Made my spouse smile .... 2,000 points
Made my spouse snicker .... 3,000 points
Made my spouse giggle .... 4,000 points
Made my spouse chuckle .... 5,000 points
Made my spouse cackle .... 6,000 points
Made my spouse belly laugh .... 7,000 points
Made my spouse howl .... 8,000 points
Made my spouse shriek .... 9,000 points
Made my spouse die laughing .... 10,000 points

_____ Her Score _____ His Score

8. Remember When. Do you have a funny story from your childhood? Even if your spouse has heard it before, share it again but this time add sound effects, gestures, or new facial expressions. How did your parents handle a note home from school? Was there ever a time you did something and got away with it? Any memories from the car as a kid? Long road trips where you all got on each other's nerves? Let some of these jog your memory:

> Remember when Dad let you sleep in the back window of the car on long trips? Now we strap the kids in like we're launching them to outer space. Seat

belts were recommended but Mom's arm was the
original airbag.

Remember when your parents stood in the kitchen
and looked out the window at you and your siblings
shooting each other with BB guns? Those were
good days.

Remember when your dad helped you build a ramp
to jump your bike over the ditch with no helmet or
pads? When you missed the jump and crashed, Dad
said, "Way to go, Son."

Remember when your dad couldn't figure out which
of your siblings was at fault, so he spanked all of ya?

Remember when Mom spanked you with whatever
she had handy?

Remember when your parents gave permission to
spank you to whomever they dropped you off with?

Those were the days your parents always sided with
the teachers. When I got a note sent home for bad
behavior, my dad never said, "Son, let me hear your
side of the story." No way. "Go to your room and
wait for me there."

Remember when you complained about what was
for dinner and then you didn't get any dinner?

Did your dad tell you the bell on the ice-cream truck meant they were out of ice cream?

Remember when your parents didn't really do much for you when you were sick? Or you faked an illness to get out of school, and Dad requested, "Throw up and prove it." If you did throw up, he said, "Now, don't you feel better? Get in the car. We are going to school." Or maybe you had a dad who waited too long to see if he could stop the bleeding before taking you to the emergency room.

Remember when your mom sang to you in the morning to wake you up? My mom is a morning person. She busted into our room in the morning, then pulled back the curtains while singing "This is the day, this is the day, that the Lord has made." Her other favorite tune was, "Rise and shine and give God the glory, glory."

Remember when your team lost and you didn't get a trophy? We played sports for the fun of it, but always declared a winner. When your team didn't make the playoffs, your parents were relieved.

Remember when you could sign your kids up for sports without committing them to tournaments in Beijing?

My attempt at humor . . .

Fell flat .... 0 points
Made my spouse smirk .... 1,000 points
Made my spouse smile .... 2,000 points
Made my spouse snicker .... 3,000 points
Made my spouse giggle .... 4,000 points
Made my spouse chuckle .... 5,000 points
Made my spouse cackle .... 6,000 points
Made my spouse belly laugh .... 7,000 points
Made my spouse howl .... 8,000 points
Made my spouse shriek .... 9,000 points
Made my spouse die laughing.................. 10,000 points

_____ Her Score _____ His Score

9. Superhero Strength. If you could choose one superhero strength, which one would you choose? Sell it to your
spouse.

- Invisibility
- Flying
- Strength
- Stretching
- Immortality
- Flame Throwing

My attempt at humor . . .

Fell flat .... 0 points
Made my spouse smirk .... 1,000 points
Made my spouse smile .... 2,000 points
Made my spouse snicker .... 3,000 points
Made my spouse giggle .... 4,000 points
Made my spouse chuckle .... 5,000 points
Made my spouse cackle .... 6,000 points
Made my spouse belly laugh .... 7,000 points
Made my spouse howl .... 8,000 points
Made my spouse shriek .... 9,000 points
Made my spouse die laughing .... 10,000 points

_____ Her Score _____ His Score

10. Ten Smiles for 10,000 points. Let's end on a high note, where you only need to see a smile. Read the following ten quick notes to your spouse out loud and fill in the blank.

1. Thank you. Thank you for _____
_____ .

2. I chose you. I still choose you because _____
_____ .

3. I love you. I love you because _____
_____ .

4. I am attracted to you. I am attracted to you most when _____.

5. I'm looking forward to growing old with you. I plan on rocking on the front porch with you and _____ _____.

6. Our kids are blessed by you. You are at your best as a parent when _____.

7. You guard our marriage. I feel our marriage is secure because _____.

8. You honor me. I feel esteemed as highly valuable when _____.

9. You make date night fun. My all-time favorite date was _____.

10. Dreaming with you pictures a special future for our marriage. I would love to one day _____.

Her score: number of smiles out of 10 _____
x 1,000 points = _____

His score: number of smiles out of 10 _____
x 1,000 points = _____

Your Final
Laughter Score

DOES THE THOUGHT of ripping a page out of a book freak you out? There are two reasons why you should rip this page out and carry it with you. First, it's easier than carrying a book around. Second, it will give you a cheat sheet to go back to those activities that nailed laughter in your relationship.

Activity	Her Score	His Score
1. Belt It Out (chapter 1)	_____	_____
2. Get Jiggy with It (chapter 1)	_____	_____
3. Laugh Therapy (chapter 2)	_____	_____
4. Tickle Yourself and Each Other (chapter 2)	_____	_____

5. Disaster Recovery (chapter 3)   _____   _____

6. Physical Humor (chapter 3)   _____   _____

7. Improv Something Easy
(chapter 4)   _____   _____

8. Improv Something
Controversial or Difficult
(chapter 4)   _____   _____

9. Aha Honor Moment
(chapter 5)   _____   _____

10. Declutter (chapter 5)   _____   _____

11. Sing It Like a Country
Song (chapter 6)   _____   _____

12. Lightning Round (chapter 7)   _____   _____

13. Would You Rather (chapter 7)   _____   _____

14. Shove Him onto
the Bed (chapter 8)   _____   _____

15. Carry Her across the
Threshold (chapter 8)   _____   _____

16. Kids Say the Darnedest
    Things (chapter 9)   _____   _____

17. Dream a Little Dream
    with Me (chapter 9)   _____   _____

18. Sixty-Second Calorie Burn
    (chapter 9)   _____   _____

19. When Was the First Time
    You Remember . . .
    (chapter 9)   _____   _____

20. Sixty Seconds of NSTs
    (chapter 9)   _____   _____

21. Lovemaking Playlist
    (chapter 9)   _____   _____

22. The Crockpot Candle
    (chapter 9)   _____   _____

23. Remember When (chapter 9)   _____   _____

24. Superhero Strength
    (chapter 9)   _____   _____

25. Ten Smiles for 10,000
    points (chapter 9)   _____   _____

Callback Journal

USE THIS PAGE to record callbacks from your marriage. See pages 3–7 to learn more about the callback.

1. _____
_____
_____
_____

2. _____
_____
_____
_____

3. _____
_____
_____
_____

4. _____
_____
_____
_____

5. _____
_____
_____
_____

6. _____
_____
_____
_____

7. _____
_____
_____
_____

8. _____
_____
_____
_____

Notes

CHAPTER 1: YOUR LAUGHTER SCORE

1. Sophie Scott, "Why We Laugh," Ted Talk (March 2015), https://www.ted.com/talks/sophie_scott_why_we_laugh.

2. Adapted from C. Kuhn, "Stages of Laughter" *Journal of Nursing Jocularity* (1994) as adapted by Berk (2001).

CHAPTER 2: THIRTY-EIGHT "WE NEED MORE OF THAT"
BENEFITS OF LAUGHTER

1. "Jeannie and Jim Gaffigan Used Humor to Cope with Her Brain Tumor," *Megan Kelly Today* (July 16, 2018), https://www.today.com/health/jeannie-jim-gaffigan-used-humor-cope-her-brain-tumor-t133326.

2. "Humor, Laughter, and Those Aha Moments," *On The Brain* 16, no. 2 (Spring 2010), https://hms.harvard.edu/sites/default/files/HMS_OTB_Spring10_Vol16_No2.pdf.

3. Ibid.

4. Karyn Buxman, "How Humor Saved the World," Tedx Talk (2017), https://www.youtube.com/watch?v=5bOriPEk7S8.

5. Steve Bhaerman, "A Sense of Humor Is a Sense of Perspective" (June 2015), https://www.linkedin.com/pulse/sense-humor-perspective-steve-bhaerman.

6. Norman Cousins, quoted in "120 Inspirational Quotes about Laughter," Laughter Online University, https://www.laughteronlineuniversity.com/120-quotes-laughter-throughout-history.

7. Henry Ward Beecher, www.famousquotesandauthors.com/authors/henry_ward_beecher_quotes.html.

8. Sophie Scott, "Why We Laugh," Ted Talk (March 2015), https://www.ted.com/talks/sophie_scott_why_we_laugh.

9. Clinton Colmenares, "No Joke: Study Finds Laughing Can Burn Calories" *Reporter* (June 6, 2005), https://www.mc.vanderbilt.edu/reporter/index.html ?ID=4030.

10. Scott, "Why We Laugh."

11. "Humor, Laughter, and Those Aha Moments," *On The Brain.*

12. Yakov Smirnoff, https://allauthor.com/quotes/212113.

13. Sophie Scott, quoted in Dr. Mercola, "10 Things You May Not Know about Laughter," *Mercola* (November 13, 2014), https://articles.mercola .com/sites/articles/archive/2014/11/13/10-fascinating-facts-laughter.aspx.

14. Reinhold Niebuhr, https://www.quotes.net/quote/74090.

15. Randy Alcorn, *Happiness* (Carol Stream, IL: Tyndale, 2015), 166.

16. Randy Alcorn, *50 Days of Heaven* (Carol Stream, IL: Tyndale, 2006), Day 43.

17. Alcorn, *Happiness*, 170.

18. Eliza E. Hewitt, "When We All Get to Heaven," pub.1898.

19. Martin Luther, quoted in Dennis Rainey, "Love and Laughter," FamilyLife (2012), https://www.familylife.com/articles/topics/marriage/staying -married/making-memories/love-and-laughter.

20. Rabbi Sydney Mintz, quoted in "120 Inspirational Quotes about Laughter," Laughter Online University, https://www.laughteronlineuniversity.com/120 -quotes-laughter-throughout-history.

21. Ethel Barrymore, quoted in "120 Inspirational Quotes about Laughter," Laughter Online University, https://www.laughteronlineuniversity.com/120 -quotes-laughter-throughout-history.

22. Mark Batterson, *Primal: A Quest for the Lost Soul of Christianity* (Colorado Springs: Multnomah, 2009), 93.

23. Mark Twain, quoted in "120 Inspirational Quotes about Laughter," Laughter Online University, https://www.laughteronlineuniversity.com/120-quotes -laughter-throughout-history.

CHAPTER 3: YOU'RE FUNNIER THAN YOU THINK

1. Peter McGraw, "What Makes Things Funny?" Tedx Talk (October 12, 2010), https://www.youtube.com/watch?v=ysSgG5V-R3U.

2. Jeffrey Hall, quoted in "Research Proves Couples That Laugh Together Are In It for the Long Haul" (February 10, 2017), https://www.huffingtonpost .ca/2017/02/10/laugh-together-relationship-couples_n_14677638.html.

3. Tripp and Tyler, "Almost Every Type of Laughing" (August 1, 2013), https://www.youtube.com/watch?v=rPY4yOmNw7w.

4. Andrew Tarvin, "The Skill of Humor," Tedx Talk (June 13, 2017), https:// www.youtube.com/watch?v=MdZAMSyn_As.

5. Roni Jacobson, "Test Yourself," The Cut (April 4, 2017), https://www .thecut.com/article/whats-your-humor-style.html.

CHAPTER 4: COO, COO, MY DOVE

1. Jack Zenger and Joseph Folkman, "What Great Listeners Actually Do," *Harvard Business Review* (July 14, 2016), https://hbr.org/2016/07/what -great-listeners-actually-do.
2. Sarah Treleaven, "The Science behind Happy Relationships," *Time* (June 26, 2018), http://time.com/5321262/science-behind-happy-healthy-relationships.
3. Ibid.
4. *Patch Adams*, directed by Tom Shadyac (Blue Wolf, 1998).

CHAPTER 5: HOLY SHIPLAP, CHIP!

1. Anne Moir and David Jessel, *Brain Sex: The Real Difference between Men and Women* (New York: A Delta Book/Dell Publishing, 1989), 9.

CHAPTER 6: EVERY MARRIAGE IS A DUET IN NEED OF GREAT BACKUP SINGERS

1. C. S. Lewis, *The Four Loves* (New York: Harcourt, 1960, 1988), 65.
2. Bella DePaulo, "Is Divorce Contagious?" *Psychology Today* (July 11, 2010), https://www.psychologytoday.com/us/blog/living-single/201007/is-divorce -contagious.
3. Ted Lowe, "Why Your Spouse Isn't Enough, and Why They Shouldn't Be," Married People website (July 9, 2018), http://marriedpeople.org/why-your -spouse-isnt-enough-and-why-they-shouldnt-be.

CHAPTER 7: FOUR HABITS OF HIGHLY HAPPY COUPLES

1. "Billy Graham Trivia: What Was Crucial to Billy and Ruth's Happy Marriage?" Billy Graham Evangelistic Association (February 8, 2017), https://billygraham.org/story/billy-graham-trivia-what-was-crucial-to -billy-and-ruths-happy-marriage.

CHAPTER 8: DON'T GET A DIVORCE, GET A DONUT

1. Maressa Brown, "How Much You Weigh Affects Your Marriage," CafeMom (July 19, 2011), http://thestir.cafemom.com/love_sex/123360/how_much _you_weigh_affects.
2. Edward Mote, "My Hope Is Built on Nothing Less," pub. 1837.
3. Peter Greer, *Mission Drift* (Bloomington, MN: Bethany House Publishers, reprint ed., 2015), 16.

CHAPTER 9: EXTRA CREDIT: TEN FAST, EASY, AND FREE WAYS TO MAKE YOUR SPOUSE LAUGH

1. These stories all came from folks at Woodland Hills Family Church, and are used here and in sermons with permission.

About the Author

TED CUNNINGHAM is the founding pastor of Woodland Hills Family Church in Branson, Missouri. He and his wife, Amy, founded the church in 2002 and have been married for over twenty-three years. They have two children, Corynn and Carson.

Ted also headlines the Date Night Comedy Tour and is a frequent conference speaker at churches and events across the country. He is a graduate of Liberty University and Dallas Theological Seminary.